REFUGIA

This is an unusual book. Combining social science fiction, utopianism, pragmatism, sober analysis, and innovative social theory, the authors address one of the biggest dilemmas of our age – how to solve the problems arising from mass displacement. As early versions of the solution proposed by Robin Cohen and Nicholas Van Hear filtered out, their vision of a new, networked, transnational archipelago, called Refugia, was met with scepticism by established refugee scholars. Others were more intrigued, more open-minded, or perhaps just holding their fire until this book was finally published. As it at least has the virtue of originality, why not judge the proposal for yourself? Read it, and craft your own critique. The authors have initiated an openly pro-refugee vision that all can help to shape. Written in a clear and direct style, this book will appeal to scholars, students, practitioners and an informed public ready to engage with this pressing issue.

Robin Cohen is professor emeritus of development studies and senior research fellow, Kellogg College, University of Oxford. His books include *The new helots: Migrants in the international division of labour* (1987, 1993, 2003), *Frontiers of identity* (1994), *Global diasporas: An introduction* (1997, 2008), *Global sociology* (co-author, 2000, 2007, 2013), *Migration and its enemies* (2006), *Encountering difference* (co-author, 2016), and *Migration: The movement of humankind from prehistory to the present day* (2019). He has edited or co-edited 21 further volumes, particularly on the sociology and politics of developing areas, diasporas, international migration, transnationalism, and globalization. He directed the International Migration Institute, part of the Oxford Martin School (2009–2011) and was principal investigator on the Oxford Diasporas Programme funded by the Leverhulme Trust (2011–2016).

Nicholas Van Hear is a researcher at the Centre on Migration, Policy and Society (COMPAS), at the University of Oxford. With a background in anthropology and development studies, he works on forced migration, conflict, development, diaspora, transnationalism, and related issues, and has field experience in Africa, the Middle East, South Asia, North America, and Europe. His books include *New diasporas: The mass exodus, dispersal and regrouping of migrant communities* (1998), *The migration-development nexus* (2003), and *Catching fire: Containing forced migration in a volatile world* (2006). His main contributions have been on force and choice in migration; migration and development; diaspora formation and engagement in conflict settings, including post-war recovery; and migration and class.

KEY IDEAS

Designed to complement the successful *Key Sociologists*, this series covers the main concepts, issues, debates, and controversies in sociology and the social sciences. The series aims to provide authoritative essays on central topics of social science, such as community, power, work, sexuality, inequality, benefits and ideology, class, family, etc. Books adopt a strong 'individual' line, as critical essays rather than literature surveys, offering lively and original treatments of their subject matter. The books will be useful to students and teachers of sociology, political science, economics, psychology, philosophy, and geography.

SERIES EDITOR: PETER HAMILTON

For a full list of titles in this series, please visit www.routledge.com/ Key-Ideas/book-series/SE0058.

REFUGIA

Radical Solutions to Mass Displacement

Robin Cohen and Nicholas Van Hear

Routledge
Taylor & Francis Group

LONDON AND NEW YORK

First published 2020
by Routledge
2 Park Square, Milton Park, Abingdon, Oxon OX14 4RN

and by Routledge
52 Vanderbilt Avenue, New York, NY 10017

Routledge is an imprint of the Taylor & Francis Group, an informa business

British Library Cataloguing-in-Publication Data
A catalogue record for this book is available from the British Library

Library of Congress Cataloging-in-Publication Data
A catalog record has been requested for this book

ISBN: 978-1-138-60155-0 (hbk)
ISBN: 978-1-138-60156-7 (pbk)
ISBN: 978-0-429-47004-2 (ebk)

Typeset in Bembo
by Lumina Datamatics Limited

CONTENTS

LIST OF FIGURES

ACKNOWLEDGEMENTS

For us, writing this book represents an important marker on an intellectual and political journey that started over four years ago. Our professional expertise is in the study of migration, especially diasporas and refugees. Confronted by the pressing issue of mass displacement, we found ourselves dismayed by how conventional solutions fell so far short of actually delivering help and support to so many desperate people. Could we help by rethinking the problem in a way that could be considered by refugees and those who work alongside them?

We started by exposing some radical ideas at a panel the Oxford Martin School convened in October 2015 and have followed this up with blog posts, short online interventions, and many presentations. We have written, and here draw on, two published articles: Robin Cohen and Nicholas Van Hear, 'Visions of Refugia: Territorial and transnational solutions to mass displacement', *Planning Theory and Practice* (2017); and Nicholas Van Hear, 'Imagining Refugia: Thinking outside the current refugee regime', *Migration and Society* (2018). At each point, we have encouraged reactions to and criticisms of our ideas, thereby allowing us to refine and develop them. A website, which can be accessed using the search term 'the Refugia project', documents these interventions and responses. Within the constraints determined by copyright issues, we intend to add reviews of this book and further responses, turning the site into an ongoing forum.

We wish to thank our students, colleagues, and people who attended our talks and presentations for their interactions and suggestions. We also need to acknowledge the vigorous peer reviews of our book proposal, to which we have tried to respond. Cathrine Brun and Anita Fábos shared with us their thinking on homemaking in its many senses. In Chapter 2, we drew on material about identity prepared by Paul Kennedy for a forthcoming book. Dace Dzenovska's work on emptiness has also influenced us, as have our many exchanges with her on the nature of politics and society. Rebecca Buxton, Giulia Gonzales, Giorgia Doná, Khachig Tölölyan, Harris Mylonas, Elisabetta Grison, Effie Voutira, Ilka Vari-Lavoisier, Louise Olliff, and many others helped us with critical readings and creative suggestions. Emre Eren Korkmaz's work on blockchains for refugees inspired one of our vignettes. Selina Molteno Cohen has read the book and improved it. Discussions with Lorraine Charles, Jason Cohen, Jonathan Tickner, Marilyn Medina Cohen, and Kate David helped to reveal holes in the argument. Some, no doubt, remain. Using his deep knowledge and experience of refugee and humanitarian organizations, Jeff Crisp has played the role of friendly critic, supplying us with a wealth of relevant material. We also thank Gerhard Boomgaarden at Routledge for his enthusiasm and for publishing an academic title that is outside the usual mould.

GLOSSARY

agora	the ancient Greek description of an open place where people gather to buy and sell, socialize, exchange ideas, and make decisions. This is the first tier of governance in a refugium q.v.
creds	short for credits, the labour points assigned to the time spent at different occupations. Creds are recorded on each Sesame Pass, q.v.
Fugee	the emerging creole spoken in many refugiums.
'fugia, fugia'	the greeting and form of recognition between Refugians.
permaconflict	the condition of persistent and extensive war worldwide.
Refugia	the name of the transnational polity organized by and for refugees and displaced people.
Refugian	or in shortened form, 'Fugian', a recognized member of Refugia, carrying a Sesame Pass, q.v.

refugium one of the many component units of Refugia, q.v.

Sesame Pass the generic name for the Sesame card, app, or chip, which provides ID and many other benefits to Refugians.

social ecotones the overlapping spaces between Somewherelands (q.v.) and refugiums (q.v.), where shared cultures and social practices emerge.

solidarian someone who offers lasting support and identifies fully with the aims of Refugia.

Somewherelands the countries within which refugiums emerge.

REFUGIA 2030

现在是2030年
أنه 1451 Hijri
It is 2030 CE.

Trends that emerged in the first part of the 2000s towards the polarization of liberal cosmopolitans and illiberal parochials have hardened. This is reflected spatially by the division of the world into metropolitan, liberal megacities with progressive administrations, often in conflict with the authoritarian national governments of the countries in which they sit: the latter's power is drawn from conservative supporters in smaller towns and the countryside.

Even more seriously, identity conflicts fuelled by ethnic, nationalist, and religious loyalties, and exacerbated by climate breakdown, continue to convulse many parts of the world, particularly a swath of territory from western China to western Africa: religious and ethno-nationalist insurgents are locked in intermittent low-level conflict that erupts into full-scale war from time to time. Big and 'emergent' powers – China, India, Russia, Europe, the United States, Brazil, Indonesia, Iran, Saudi Arabia, and others – continue to be dragged into many-sided proxy wars.

Commentators term this condition as 'permaconflict', and millions of displaced people are on the move as a result.

More positively, a transnational polity called *Refugia* is consolidating itself after a shaky start following the failure of the Global Compacts on Refugees and Migration that were meant to regulate and make safe the movement of migrants and refugees. Beginning as a global socio-political movement agitating to resolve mass displacement, Refugia is not a new nation-state, but rather a transnational or cross-national entity. Confederal in character, the best analogy is with a loosely connected archipelago that brings together hundreds of refugee communities in many territories, be they in neighbouring societies or in more distant countries of settlement. Refugia is in part spontaneously fashioned and in part the outcome of a grand bargain – between richer states and 'emergent' countries, countries neighbouring conflict zones, and, crucially, refugees themselves.

The constituent territories of Refugia are in effect licensed – or at least tacitly tolerated – by the nation-states or local authorities within whose territories they lie. A collective name for such hosts has been coined by some refugees. *Somewhereland*, they call it – a pointed way of defining places that have encouraged refugee settlement or, at least, tolerated their presence.[1] While not according refugees full citizenship or even processing most of their asylum claims, some south European, African, west Asian, and South American states have taken an early lead in accommodating one or more *refugiums* (components of the trans-national collectivity Refugia). Small, local communities and many municipal administrations of liberal-run megacities have done likewise – sometimes against the wishes of the authoritarian nation-states in which they lie. There are now, in 2030, over 300 refugiums worldwide.

Governance

Refugia has some of the symbols of trans-nationhood, having adopted the flag and the anthem of a 'Refugee Nation', designed and composed by Syrian refugees in 2018. However, at the heart of Refugia are self-governing constituent components, which Refugians confidently proclaim will eventually be self-supporting. Refugia as a whole is governed by a transnational virtual assembly, elected by Refugians from all the constituent components of the polity. Periodic face-to-face refugee assemblies have also been convened, the first in Europe (2018), with subsequent parliaments in Asia, Africa, and the Americas. These overarching structures represent Refugia globally, but there are also constituent assemblies in each refugium that feed into this global representation, as well as represent the interests of Refugians to their particular host society – and also channel the concerns of the host society to Refugians.

Refugians hold multiple belongings: they can move among different parts of Refugia, and, where negotiated, between those Somewherelands that are sovereign nations or common travel areas. This is facilitated by the *Sesame Pass*, which encrypts the entitlements that Refugians hold.[2] Many Refugians are also citizens or recognized residents of the Somewhereland states that license their territories, in which case they are subject to the laws of both Refugia and the Somewhereland host state. Some Refugians live in discrete territories or spaces; others live side by side with Somewherelanders, especially in large, metropolitan cities.[3] The upshot is that refugees are no longer primarily the responsibility of the Somewhereland nation-state that 'hosts' them, but of a more diffuse entity – Refugia.

Interestingly, a considerable number of citizens of Somewhereland 'host' societies have become Refugians by choice, where local assemblies have accepted their applications. When interviewed, those who have become elective Refugians have said they seek alternative forms of living to those in authoritarian democracies that hold sway in much of the world. Therefore, as well as those displaced by conflict, Refugia attracts the left-outs of neo-illiberalism, just as authoritarian democracies appealed to and incorporated the left-behinds of neo-liberal globalization from the 2010s.

Economy

Refugia's economy builds on the skills of Refugians in cultural and creative industries, education, and digital commerce and services and is based on the proliferation of various kinds of distance work. Some employment has been negotiated in special Refugee Economic Zones located between Refugia and Somewhereland.[4] Also by mutual agreement, some Refugians can work in Somewhereland proper, with agreed proportions of tax revenue having been negotiated by the two polities. However, as Refugia becomes more autonomous economically, this kind of dependent work is diminishing. Refugia as a whole is at the forefront of innovations under the aegis of Global Green, the successor to the Green Emergency Deal, which two-thirds of the world's countries signed up to in the early 2020s.

Substantial portions of the stock of housing and commercial property are held in trust by Refugia to accommodate and provide workspaces for the 'churn' of Refugians passing through different parts of Refugia over time or moving on to Somewherelands that have admitted them. In keeping with Global Green, the stock of Refugians in any one refugium is determined by a 'Capacity Rating', derived from an algorithm negotiated with the host society. Devised by Refugian digital specialists wary of covert control by the technology corporations, the algorithm includes such elements as local housing stock, employment and self-employment numbers, ecological impact assessments, and various demographic indicators that support the liberal provisions of Refugia's progressive outlook. In most cases, the agreed Capacity Rating has obviated the need for a repressive immigration policy.

Refugians pay some taxes or contributions to the nation-states within which they live, but also to the wider Refugia polity. A portion of the latter revenue provides support for those who choose to stay in their regions of origin – in a similar manner to the way in which remittances have been deployed. Taxes also provide a means of cross-subsidy among differently endowed parts of Refugia.

Overall character

Refugia at large is not based on ethnicity, nationality, or religion. Permaconflict has convinced many people of the fallacy of basing communities on narrowly defined identifications. Inevitably, some heritage identities still persist in vestigial form. However, Refugians have of necessity been pressed into collective activity across such affiliations by their experience of forced movement, the hostility of some host governments, and the process of building new communities. Differences are respected, but Refugians have been driven by their everyday challenges to create a new kind of polity that is democratic, self-sustaining, and forward-looking – and not based on identity politics.

Since Refugia has been formed cumulatively and incrementally, the confederal transnational polity has been able to experiment with forms of inter-governmental relations and economy to see what works and what does not. In terms of borders, most of the constituent units of Refugia have negotiated a porous border with surrounding host states, slowly and incrementally moving goods, information, and people between old political borders without disrupting long-held territorial identities. Some have created 'social ecotones' (mutually accessed public spaces). This gradual evolution of zones where different ethnicities cohabited became necessary when trials of completely open borders triggered outbreaks of violence by xenophobes in the illiberal nation-states.

In terms of economy, parts of Refugia are at the forefront of post-capitalist global utopian experiments to supplant actually existing capitalism. Some have tried out peer-to-peer, sharing economies and horizontal forms of sociality, which seek to prefigure a post-capitalist networked society and green economy – based on production and distribution of information and knowledge rather than market-based relations.[5] Other parts go along with conventional capitalism – though of a Social Democratic, welfarist kind – unlike the neo-liberal and authoritarian variants of capitalism that still are found in many Somewherelands. (As mentioned, some Refugians reluctantly work in a number of economic zones located in the ecotones between Refugia and Somewhereland.)

In sum, Refugia is a pragmatic arrangement, a kind of secession by mutual agreement. For their part, authoritarian and illiberal states see it as in their interest to shuffle off the issue of displacement to the displaced themselves, while the displaced and those seeking an alternative to authoritarianism relish the prospect of a self-managed new society that they create by and for themselves. As Refugians readily concede, they certainly do not currently live in Utopia, but this has not prevented them from dreaming utopian dreams and making plans for a better future for themselves and their children.

Notes

1 We are not quite sure, but suspect that the name Somewhereland is an ironic nod to Goodhart (2017), who, in his analysis of the appeal of populism, saw the world as divided between 'Anywheres' (liberal, rootless metropolitans) and 'Somewheres' (grounded provincial folk deeply committed to places in small towns and the countryside). It is instructive that that the refugee activists who coined the word 'Somewhereland' avoided the terms Anywhereland or Nowhereland, despite the fact that the social construction of Refugia has drawn on utopian thinking. In this respect, we note that the original meaning of utopia was 'no place', and that William Morris's most famous utopian tract was titled *News from Nowhere* (1890). Refugians clearly want to be somewhere!

2 The *Sesame Pass* is available as an app, while subcutaneous chips and even old-fashioned cards are offered. Based on platforms independent of the big tech corporations, they provide a secure digital identity, access to entitlements, the means of participation in governance, and support many other aspects of Refugia membership. The functions of an early model Sesame card were first outlined by two friends of Refugia, Cohen and Van Hear (2017). The name derived from the expression 'open Sesame' (Arabic: سمسم يا إفتــــح) used in the Arab folk tale, Ali Baba, showing the way to a cave of treasures. The principal treasures Refugians seek are security and dignity. One might note in passing that the Chinese retail giant, Alibaba, has also appropriated the Arab folk tale to develop a 'Sesame Credit score' for its customers, a rather different exercise.

3 Literary critics have noticed that in this respect, Refugia is in some ways a benevolent version of China Miéville's dystopian novel *The City and the City* (2011) and also resonates with Mohsin Hamid's novel *Exit West* (2017).

4 These were first proposed by Alexander Betts and Paul Collier (2017) and have proved a means of providing employment in some cases, though there have been persistent complaints of exploitation by employers.

5 These Refugians are 'new historical subjects', akin to Paul Mason's (2015) fully networked individuals.

1

INTRODUCTION

Mass displacement is one of the most pressing global issues of our time. Many more people are being driven from their homes: more than 70 million people worldwide were forcibly displaced by the end of 2018, including nearly 26 million refugees (over half of whom were under 18), 41 million internally displaced people, and 3.5 million asylum seekers (UNHCR 2019). The overall figure has been on an upward trend for most of the last decade or more. A large number of migrants and refugees are dying en route to safety each year – over 5,000 people perished trying to cross the Mediterranean in 2016 alone. Several thousand Rohingya were killed when nearly a million of them fled Myanmar by land or sea. Meanwhile, more than 3.7 million people have fled from Venezuela, the majority of whom are considered to need international protection. Evidence that displaced peoples' needs are being met is thin on the ground: only 92,400 refugees were resettled in 2018 (UNHCR 2019). The unambiguous message of these figures is testimony in itself to the scale of the problem of mass displacement.

In addition to the bald statistical indictment of how poorly the global community is dealing with the issue, we can add three further comments:

- Few have confidence that the three conventional 'durable solutions' (local integration, resettlement, and return) offered by the refugee agencies can address the challenge on the scale needed. There are serious limits and constraints – not least economic, ecological, institutional, and political – that militate against realization of these 'durable solutions'
- Those institutions and sections of civil society that support tolerant attitudes towards refugees and asylum seekers, respect for humanitarian rights, law and principles, and internationalism are under fierce attack from right-wing and populist forces in many countries
- While many governments have pulled back from refugee-friendly policies, some have gone a step further in openly abrogating their legal obligations. For example, in January 2018, the European Union referred three of its member states to the European Court of Justice for refusing to process asylum applications. The Czech Republic had accepted only 12 of the 2,000 asylum seekers it had been assigned, while Hungary and Poland had processed none at all. In September 2017, President Trump slashed by over half, the number of planned refugee admissions to the US.

Jeff Crisp (2018) has pointed to another looming crisis – funding. By April 2018, the United Nations High Commission for Refugees (UNHCR) had received only US\$2.3 billion of the US\$8.2 billion it estimated it needed for its annual work. Shortly after, Trump's administration announced massive cuts to the United Nations Relief and Works Agency (UNRWA) which supports five million Palestinian refugees in the Occupied Territories, Lebanon, Jordan, and Syria, describing it as an 'irredeemably flawed operation'. As the US contribution is 40 per cent of the total, cuts to the main UNRWA budget will have a devastating effect. As Crisp (2018) notes, the funding crisis has thrown the UNHCR at large into the arms of the EU and its member states, who have 'have shown little hesitation in violating the international refugee laws they have signed in their desperation to seal Europe's borders'.

In short, it has become increasingly evident that the international institutional architecture set up to address mass displacement and find solutions for it is simply unequal to the task at hand. The refugee and migration summits in the US in September 2016 rounded off no fewer than seven major international meetings convened in that year to provide long-term solutions to the refugee and migrant crisis. Indeed, 2016 was dubbed 'the Year of Summits'. Perhaps the most ambitious plan emerging from this series of international meetings was the New York Declaration for Refugees and Migrants, adopted in September 2016. This involved an undertaking to work towards 'Global Compacts' for refugees and for safe, orderly, and regular migration, eventually agreed at the end of 2018. However, with swingeing UN budget cuts as a result of President Trump's displeasure with the body, it is difficult to see much practical result emerging from this series of summits and the Global Compacts. The US has formally renounced its commitment to the UN-led Global Compact for Safe, Orderly, and Regular Migration, while Austria, Australia, Bulgaria, Chile, Croatia, the Czech Republic, Dominican Republic, Estonia, Hungary, Italy, Israel, Latvia, Poland, Slovakia, and Switzerland did not show up to the conference in Morocco finalizing the agreement and most are unlikely to sign it.

The word 'failure' is a harsh one and many of those with whom we interact insist that it remains important to defend international law (particularly the 1951 Refugee Convention and associated protocols designed to protect refugees), to press states and international organizations to take their moral and legal obligations seriously and, through the force of popular mobilization, turn the tide of anti-migrant and anti-refugee public opinion. We wholeheartedly concur, but advance two additional, but essential, arguments. The first is a simple entreaty – 'not only, but also'. Carrying on doing what we (the international community and those who wish to support refugees) have been doing since 1945 is a worthy aim, but not enough. Given the scale of the problem, we need to do more, much more. We need to reach for imaginative, alternative, and supplementary solutions. The second argument is that the 'we' has to be extended well beyond the circle of progressive activists, international agencies, humanitarian organizations, and sympathetic officials, to refugees themselves, seeing them as agents and empowering 'them' to act on their own behalf, with an embold-ened sense of identity and purpose. Although the agentic refugee has now become a frequent evocation in theory and policy, practice lags far behind. The old 'we' needs to move beyond mere paternalism and virtue signalling to concrete acts of solidarity.

The authors of this book are not alone in suggesting that a radi-cal rethinking of how to address the problem of mass displacement is now necessary. This book both evaluates current alternative proposals and sets outs our own ideas. Our proposal has been projected into an imagined future in the preface that opens this book. In brief, our plan is to encourage the formation of a new entity, which we desig-nate 'Refugia'. Refugia is not a state, nor a conventional international organization, but combines elements of both. Refugia is not based in a single territory, rather it comprises *hundreds* of sites or locales, strung out along a networked archipelago. (These sites can be camps, agricul-tural settlements, safe zones, hostels, or neighbourhoods – wherever displacees have congregated or been gathered.) Refugia is governed highly democratically. If you have been displaced, you can sign up. You can join freely and leave freely. Through digital means, Refugians will participate in democratic elections and referenda. They will draw up demands, run campaigns, and advance legal claims. Refugians will have the capacity to press for improvements to their lives and gain access to resources they require. Friends of Refugia ('solidarians') will be able to offer support and entitlements and engage in shared initia-tives with Refugians.

All this is unconventional and difficult to take in at one gulp, so we need to proceed sip by sip. In Chapter 2, we explain how new and reworked political and social theory – about the state, liquidity, identity formation, deterritorialization, homemaking, the commons, and utopianism – can shift our mind-sets away from taken-for-granted assumptions about the global political order and the persistent, but misguided assumption that only nation-states matter.

As mentioned, others have suggested that radical or 'lateral' thinking to address the issue of mass displacement needs to be deployed. Some of this new thinking emanates from within the international organizations supporting refugees, some comes from concerned academics, and a few proposals originate from concerned mavens who have drawn on their expertise and experience. In Chapter 3, the most prominent alternative schemes and visions are considered, including those emanating from scholars with long-held expertise, and more unconventional interventions – proposing a 'refugee nation', 'refugee islands', 'refugee/sanctuary cities', or wholly new social formations.

We argue that however radical our own proposal may appear, there are precedents and current examples of self-organization by refugees that prefigure and exemplify the possibility and potential of Refugia (Chapter 4). Some of the experiments in self-organization have been halting and insufficient, but, we argue, there is still something we can learn from prior attempts at homemaking and community building.

Having reviewed other ideas and practices, we move, in Chapter 5, to the level of praxis, seeking to apply, realize, and operationalize our vision of Refugia. We show how ethnic and religious differences can be mitigated, how relationships with surrounding host states can be negotiated, and how political representation and democratic choices can be maximized. We also describe how the economy and security of each refugium can be optimized. Finally, we spell out how the issue of a special smart card/app/chip, designated a *Sesame Pass*, might work in practice. We include a discussion about the potential and limitations of block chain technology to animate some of the objectives of Refugia.

Our final chapter summarizes the argument, engages with some of our critics, and seeks to persuade readers that our proposal to build a transnational polity, Refugia, is an attainable way forward.

VIGNETTE (2030)

The gong sounds at the Janat Refugium (Registered No. 920/2022), Somewhereland in North Africa

The gong sounded.

'I declare the weekly agora of Janat open', said the new presiding officer. 'As we have decided in earlier meetings the agora will finish when the gong sounds in one and half hours, with all unfinished business to go to the next meeting.'

The agora was held in the old market square, still filled with the impressive cut stones of the Cyrene period. Along the edge, xeric pines had doggedly survived with one tall specimen dominating the centre, where most of the discussion took place.

The agora had adapted an old Swahili proverb to describe their vibrant democracy: 'Fugians sit under the tree and talk until they agree'.

At first, it was routine business. The wells were fine, but the desalination filters were again clogging up with salt. It was agreed to ask the Janat science cluster to investigate using the older, but more reliable, ceramic models. Meanwhile two more volunteers for filter cleaning were needed – 20 labour points (creds) per day would be added to each worker's Sesame account.

Two young members shyly put their hands up. 'We will offer,' they said. Everyone could see they were in love and no doubt they thought they could find a little privacy at the desalination plant. They'd soon find out it isn't such great fun – the salt is corrosive and sometimes a flake would get in their eyes.

The next business was more controversial. The refugium's Capacity Rating (CR) was 1,400 people, including all children. The attendees decided to confirm the CR until such time as fresh water supplies could be significantly boosted.

This left places for just 25 people and suddenly the meeting became heated. Ten places were quickly assigned to pregnant women already in Janat, but 'sponsors' then passionately argued for their nominees.

Patrice spoke first: 'My cousin has been tortured in her country.' He tapped the Sesame chip in his arm and the gruesome photos appeared as holograms. Five more, with her family. Other deserving cases followed, and some in the agora had tears in their eyes, remembering the sufferings they had endured.

Finally, they considered the cases of two solidarians, Ebba and Lars. They had been there in the bad old days pulling displaced people from the sea when the people smugglers had cut them adrift. Now they offered legal and social work services in Arabic and English. Their applications to join Janat as full members were greeted enthusiastically. This was both a popular and well-timed decision, as a few seconds later the gong sounded.

Everyone dispersed, talking softly, the turpentine smell of the pine lingering.

2

THINKING DIFFERENTLY

Political and social theory

It is hard to think beyond our taken-for-granted assumptions. For many people, states, or more elusively, 'nation-states' define the political order of the world. However, we submit that it is important to focus on the other structures in which power is organized. Again, it is often thought that social identities inhere in national identities. Certainly, we may be Malians, Italians, Australians, or Sri Lankans. However, is that all we are? Or are identities also now formed in more complex, 'liquid' ways, not predicated on national affinities? Do polities and other social formations have to be bounded by definite territorial frontiers? Alternatively, in a digital age, can we imagine a new kind of *polis*, a set of communities located in multiple spaces linked through electronic means? The imagined world of nation-states privileges sedentary norms and territories, but the world is increasingly on the move. Should we be thinking of more loosely defined spaces like archipelagos or a 'mobile commons'? Should homemaking, often involving shifts in gender relations, be understood not as permanent settlement, but as a contingent, iterative process undertaken many times over as people move from pillar to post? Again, given the extent and increase of mass displacement, should we be seeking fresh solutions and new ways of understanding how to organize societies? For this to happen, we need 'utopian thinking', an expression which, we argue below, needs to be liberated from derogatory common-sense understandings and used in a much more analytical and methodological way. We address these questions in turn below.

Beyond the nation-state

In mid-2019, the United Nations (UN) recognized 193 states. This bare statement needs immediate qualification. Two states, the Holy See and the State of Palestine, only have observer-state status at the UN. Some member states do not recognize all members of the UN; certain states not recognized by the UN are recognized by some states; and two non-UN-states are only recognized by other non-UN-recognized states. And Somaliland is recognized by no one but itself. Such complications are easily dismissed as mere idiosyncrasies. However, we can begin to intuit that perhaps states are not quite as intrinsic to the natural order as is commonly supposed. For a start, they are quite recent inventions. Historians date the formal creation of states to the 1648 Peace of Westphalia marking the end of European wars of religion, but nearly three-quarters of the UN members came into existence after the Second World War. They are grossly uneven in wealth and power, and the Gross National Products (GNPs) of many states are lower than the valuations of the top band of global corporations.

When it comes to 'nation-states', the picture gets murkier. Are all states made up of only one nation? Clearly not, as (to confine ourselves for the moment to Europe) the Bretons, Catalans, Scots, and Corsicans forcibly remind us of from time to time. The proliferation of studies on multiculturalism, diversity, ethnicity, and nationalism is a clear indicator that the congruence or conjunction of state, nation, social identity, and territory is highly problematic. Despite this, many social scientists stumble into the trap of what Wimmer and Glick Schiller (2002) call 'methodological nationalism', a naïve assumption that only nation-states matter as units of analysis. To understand our idea of Refugia, methodological nationalism has to be rejected tout court. The nation-state is merely an ideological and political *project*, never fully realized and always contested.

A richer starting point is to assume that nation-states are but one 'power container' among many, what Giddens (1985: 13) termed 'circumscribed arenas for the generation of administrative power'. But there are other containers, other arenas, and other forms of power. To take three obvious examples, outside and often above the state are global corporations, global religions, and even multiply located wealthy individuals:

- The turn of the year 2009/2010 marked the moment when, of the 120 most important economic units in the world, fewer were nation-states (59) than global corporations (61) (Cohen and Kennedy 2013: 181–4). Is it any wonder that many powerful corporations evade tax, suborn politicians, and mock the sovereignty of nation-states by legal manoeuvres and accounting tricks?
- Global religions compete for spiritual adherents, but they have massive political influence too, and, not incidentally, are also substantial economic units. The Catholic Church alone owns 177 million acres worldwide (Cahill 2006), a clutch of non-contiguous territories that easily exceeds the size of mainland France.
- Oxfam calculated that by 2018, the world's 42 richest people commanded the same wealth as the poorer half of the world (Elliott 2018). In their global reach and influence, such individuals, with their entourages, foundations, and camp-followers, are like the kings and emperors of old, though transposed to a global stage.

A little historical perspective also does not come amiss. Empires, caliphates, diasporas, powerful city-states, and trade networks all preceded nation-states, then co-existed with them. Formal empires may have gone, while an Islamic caliphate fuelled by hate and violence has been defeated. However, global cities, diasporas, and trade networks are gaining new traction in the contemporary period. The last include criminal gangs (trafficking drugs, illegal goods and people), as well as those organizing legitimate commerce. Other important power containers comprise international governmental and non-governmental organizations. By 2012, there were 5,000 international governmental organizations and 25,000 international non-governmental organizations (UIA 2012/3). Regional organizations, some like the European

Union with supra-state aspirations, also abound. Many more informal networks, operating above and below the level of individual countries, are now linked by the web – which itself has largely escaped state control.

The point of all these illustrations is not to abolish the nation-state as a category or deny that a considerable number of nation-states remain powerful centres of power. Rather, we want to make much more visible the plethora of other ways – political, economic, social, and digital – in which power is now organized. Seen in this way, Refugia, though an audacious idea, is neither deviant nor bizarre, merely another power container that can operate alongside (between, within, outside) nation-states and the many other centres of power we have identified.

Deterritorializing the nation

What has gone wrong with the classic idea of the nation-state? By the end of the twentieth century, clinging on to a territorial expression of a national identity had become more and more implausible. It has now reached its historical limits. There are many examples of the problematic outcomes of the old assumption that national identities needed territorial expression. Take the case of Israel. Teodor Herzl, the founder of political Zionism, lamented that Jews had vainly sought to assimilate to the nations around them, and so had been forced into becoming a nation. 'The enemy has made us one without our desiring it', he said. But, he continued, 'we do have the strength to create a state' (Goldberg and Raynor 1989: 166). The scattered remnants of European Jewry that remained after the Holocaust, not to mention the many Jews who experienced discrimination or persecution subsequently, had every reason to be thankful for the existence of the Israeli state. In many cases, it saved their lives and assured their futures.

However, it does not follow that Israel provides a model for other aspiring nations. As Shlaim (2000) compellingly argues, for the Israeli state, security behind 'an iron wall' became more important than peace with the Arabs. The consequence was the humiliation, scattering, and dispossession of the Palestinians. Paradoxically, despite this deleterious experience, the Palestinian leadership held firmly to the lodestar of 'a state' – though finally endorsing the principle of 'two states for two peoples'. At the conclusion of the Oslo Accords of 1993, Palestinian 'statehood' had been reduced to two non-contiguous territories – the West Bank (over 40 per cent of which is now occupied by Jewish settlements) and the Gaza strip, separated from the West Bank by Israel. What remains is a pitiful shadow of the Palestinian leaders' original aspirations. Moreover, the two-state solution has been further frustrated by the Israeli government's control of people seeking to move between the territories and its refusal even to recognize the Palestinian state, flying in the face of the 136 members of the UN who have accorded Palestine that status.

For a long time, the temptation of a territorialized statehood also enthralled the Kurds, cheated, as they were, by the victors' carve up of the Middle East after the First World War. Scattered across southeastern Turkey, northern Iraq, northwestern Iran, and northern Syria, Kurds have had a bumpy ride in their century-old struggle for statehood. The proxy and civil wars in Syria and the collapse of the Islamic State caliphate have given Kurdish nationalists renewed hope of an independent state defended by the military facts on the ground. However, these realities also include the fact that the Turkish govern-ment has intervened militarily to prevent an emergent Kurdistan act-ing as a base to support the Kurdish Workers Party (PKK), which the Turkish regime regards as a terrorist group. In addition, the Kurds are not united around a common goal. While many in the Kurdish dias-pora lament their statelessness, some want greater autonomy in existing states, thus abjuring a pan-Kurdish one-state ideology. As Eliassi (2016: 1415) found, 'Kurds in [the] diaspora do not necessarily or uncritically embrace the idea of Kurdish statehood when the state cannot guaran-tee democracy, [the] rule of law and effective citizenship', while some resist the idea of a state on the grounds that it evinces too narrow an ethno-political identity.

We have suggested that the territorial nation-state may have reached its historical limits as an organizing political category. The most glaring example of this is South Sudan, the 193rd member of the UN. There were, at first sight, compelling reasons to create a new state – a long history of civil war, Muslim–Christian antago-nisms, and the possibility of using oil revenues to fund the neophyte state, which attained independence in 2011. Within two years a rolling civil war erupted, which so far has resulted in the displacement of nearly two million people (a sixth of the population), many in response to genocidal threats, mass rape, and brutal violence. As de Waal (2014) has observed, the state started as a corrupt, militarized kleptocracy, then when oil production was halted (initially as a bargaining chip), things got even worse. There was not enough money to fund the insatiable greed of the warlords and political bosses, who saw statehood merely as an opportunity for personal aggrandizement. With South Sudan at the top of the Fragile States Index, it is perhaps hardly surprising that the UN is not keen to accord recognition to the roughly 78 'nations' (obviously this description is both an approximation and a disputable category) wishing to gain recognition as a territorial state. Nevertheless, as Keating (2018) shows, such 'not-quite-country entities' and would-be nations that do not fit the conventional nation-state order are pervasive worldwide today.

From nations to liquid identities

Although ardent nationalists continue to assert the dominant or exclusive role of the nation and nation-state in defining group identities, many social identities have escaped the confines of the nation altogether and become both more personalized and more multiple. An identity is no longer a given, assumed, monolithic, naturalized condition. Rather, it can be self-chosen, tactically deployed and complex, often combining past and present identities, as well as elements of conformity and deviance. Similar processes are at work in many group interactions. Group identities are socially constructed and derived from shared sufferings and achievements, quotidian struggles, and collective plans for a future together. Plotting a future together is generally easier if social actors have something in common – a phenotype, religion, language, or ethnicity being the most obvious. We will call these commonalities 'heritage identities', always remembering that the past is itself a pliable reconstruction of the present (Lowenthal 1985).

Despite their importance, heritage identities are not the end of the story. People of different backgrounds may, and do, choose to belong together despite being attached to their differences. Rather than seeking to elide or suppress differences – the crude tactic of old-fashioned nationalists – advocates of what may be loosely called civic nationalism seek to embrace pluralism through recognition, acceptance, negotiation, and reconciliation (Bauman 2000: 177–8). Heritage identities may also fade into the distance in some settings. In their study of how new social identities are formed, Cohen and Sheringham (2016) show how, through habituation or conscious choice, migrants are able to combine traces of a diasporic past with contemporary interactions involving host and other migrant communities. The result is a continuous process of hybridization and creolization, the melding, making, and remaking of new identities.

To a much more limited degree, this fusion process gained recognition in earlier discourses, notably in the idea of 'hyphenated Americans' – Polish-Americans, Italian-Americans, African Americans (without the hyphen), and the like. But the formulation was much too static and circumscribed. Only two identities were acknowledged (one original ethnicity and one national affiliation). Nowadays, multiple ethnicities often replace one or two, while diverse gender identities (bi, gay, lesbian, trans, and inter) frequently replace heteronormativity. Dual nationals are common (50 countries now permit this), while long-established religious convictions are challenged by secularism, syncretism, agnosticism, or self-fashioned forms of spirituality. Again, hyphenated identities characteristically only allowed heritage to comprise the first part of the fused identity in the private sphere and in socially sanctioned cultural spaces. The second part, the -British, -American, or -Australian identity, required conformity in political matters. This simple bifurcation of identity is no longer adequate.

Contemporary forms of belonging are predicated less on long-established national or ethnic loyalties and more on a multitude of small-scale interactions and reactions in everyday life – in the street, at school, in the workplace, or at home. Identity is also made, remade, and altered by participation in public events and rituals like attending weddings, watching the World Cup, praying in a church or temple, or going to a music festival.

We can add one more component to this emergent picture. For many people, fixed ascribed identities (ethnic, racial, gendered, religious, or national) are increasingly seen as irritating, irrelevant, or even oppressive.

Chosen lifestyles have augmented or substituted for traditional ways of classifying people. What clothes one wears, what music one appreciates, what sport one follows, what online games one plays, what friends one has garnered through social media, whether one is able-bodied, or manages a disability – these and related forms of social engagement increasingly determine a good part of one's social identity.

We live in what Bauman (2007) suggestively calls 'liquid times', a fluid, ever-shifting set of alliances, affinities, and preferences. Does that mean that those who express an unalloyed national identity no longer exist? Of course not. We only have to look at those who propelled President Trump to office or voted for the UK to leave the European Union to see the continuing force of hard core nationalism. Such voters are easily dismissed as the 'left-behinds', and in a sense that is true. Footloose capital, its concentration in global cities and environmental choices (favouring electric cars and green energy over gas guzzlers and coal) have marooned older citizens, together with those living in rural areas and industrial rustbelts. But they are 'left-behinds' in another sense – still clinging to an outdated idea of a nation, a solid identity associated with patriotism, a flag, a territory, and sufficient military clout to defend it all. Others have moved on, adjusting to the new, complex, mobile (though often threatening and uncertain) world we inhabit. 'Moving on' means one no longer expects a simple reply to a question like 'where do you come from?', and many people have learned not to ask. They do not ask, since the answer is often laden with ambiguity, longing, nostalgia, apprehension, and intricacy.

The uncertainty surrounding contemporary social identities arises from the core idea that identity construction is never complete, it is always in process. Moreover, if we think arithmetically – that is in terms of addition, subtraction, and substitution – addition is the overwhelmingly popular choice. Thus, people can synchronously be refugees, asylum seekers, gay, Muslim, Syrians, Germans, flexitarians, opera-lovers, football fans, and many other things beside. In liquid times, such fluid identities and affinities are not only mutually incompatible, but are also increasingly normal. This is in marked contrast to older forms of social identity that demanded exclusive loyalty to a single nation or a taken-for-granted religion, usually one inherited from one's parents. At the extreme end of social constructivism, social identity dissolves into consumer choice, rather like moving along the shelves of a supermarket and chucking various identity goods into one's personalized trolley. In practice, necessity, contingency, and the weight of heritage identities will limit, though not fully determine, the choice on offer.

How does this argument apply to displaced people who find themselves in camps, detention centres, and run-down neighbourhoods, usually a long way from home? They will no doubt retain elements of distinct heritage identities that remain as memories and identity markers, though these will become more vestigial in time. Given the pattern of displacement, at first, these markers will be apparent. The majority ethnic populations among the displacees in Bangladesh are Rohingyas, in Dadaab, they are Somalis, while in Lebanon, they are Syrians of various ethnic backgrounds. However, the very fact that they are placeless people gives them something in common with displacees from other heritages, more likely than not sharing the horror of war, the trauma of displacement, the sufferings of the journey, rejection at border-posts, the harshness of people smugglers and police forces, and the everyday struggles to survive. Their common travails will provide an important backdrop to the social construction of a new collective identity. However, unlike those in a fortunate enough position to claim totally elective and freely selected social identities, Refugians will first have to cope with the dead weight of necessity – ensuring their safety, queuing for water, food, and medicines, patching up their shelters, looking after the elderly and sick, and maintaining their hopes for a better life.

These limiting conditions will mean that many displacees will initially be preoccupied by creating a viable *oikos* (a Greek word, roughly meaning a household or immediate neighbourhood). As the eminent political philosopher Hannah Arendt argued, in ancient Greece, women and slaves were locked into the *oikos* by the need to reproduce the requirements of life. The *polis* was where adult Greek men could pursue an active, fulfilling, and participatory political life (see Lechte 2018: 5). For Arendt, the *oikos–polis* dichotomy illustrated the way in which political theory could best mirror the dichotomy between necessity and freedom. We are persuaded by her argument up to this point, but she goes on to maintain that the only means whereby the stateless of the twentieth century could overcome their dire condition was to become members of the modern functional equivalent of a Greek *polis*, that is, citizens in an existing nation-state.

We beg to differ on this point. Such an option is rapidly disappearing for twenty-first-century displacees. Now tens of millions of marginalized people are having to make a life for themselves in difficult conditions outside the gilded cages inhabited by established citizenries in recognized nation-states. The construction of their social identities is determined by *neither* being able to go back, *nor* being able to anticipate acceptance into an existing nation-state. The force of the 1951 Refugee Convention was predicated on keeping these two options open. Instead, we have a condition of limbo that can easily collapse into purgatory, oblivion, and a fateful passivity, a long-term sordid *oikos*.

We argue that the construction of a positive identity has to go beyond the diminishing hopes of acceptance into an existing nation-state and beyond collective suffering and victimhood. An alternative trajectory requires a Herculean exercise of political will, a purposive movement to develop collective plans for a future together, involving self-representation and self-organization. We might wish to proclaim the outcome as 'a nation' or better a 'trans-nation'. This labelling is less important than recognizing that collective suffering *combined* with aspirations can produce the social glue that will allow a new type of *polis* to be constructed. This multiply located '*panpolis*' is what we call Refugia.

Archipelagos and ecotones

We advance the idea that it is now time to think beyond the idea of the territorial state in favour of digitally connected *archipelagos* and shared spaces called *ecotones*, both of which require explication. For some, the word 'archipelago' has a sinister reputation derived from Solzhenitsyn's (1986) description of the Siberian labour camps as *The Gulag Archipelago*, where Soviet political dissidents were disciplined. By contrast, the archipelago we envision is more wondrous and benign, somewhat like constellations of stars. Well, maybe not quite so sublime. Our core idea is derived from the Caribbean cultural theorist, Édouard Glissant (1997), who entreats us to engage in 'archipelagic thinking'.

For him, as Bongie (1999: 89) explains, 'the entire world is becoming an archipelago … actual archipelagos such as the Caribbean are exemplary sites for understanding the complex new relations that ambivalently and chaotically join together all the hitherto unconnected parts of the world'. Glissant calls this process of linking Relation (with a capital R). As Bongie (2009: 94) elsewhere clarifies – partly citing Glissant – Relation ties, but does not bind, the self to the other, the excluded to the included, and the nation to the stranger:

> That is why Glissant consistently refers to an aesthetics or poetics, as opposed to a politics, of Relation. He is adamant that no solution to the problems of the world will be lasting, or even beneficial for any length of time, without being preceded by an enormous insurrection of the imaginary, one that will prompt les humanités to wish to be and to create themselves as what they are in reality: namely, 'un changement qui ne finit pas, dans une perennité qui ne se fige pas' [an altering that never ends, in a perennial state of unsettling].

This 'insurrection of the imaginary' undermines the normativity of the nation-state. Instead, archipelagic thinking allows us to interweave transnational threads and networks, rhizomes and epiphytes, diasporas and epistemic communities, fans and friends, and nodes and edges. And, of course, with the aid of an archipelagic imagination, we can usefully envision the components and connections of the transnational archipelago that will make up and continually refashion our vision for the displaced, Refugia.

Archipelagic and Relational thinking have been made directly relevant to the issue of mass displacement by Glissant's fellow Martinican cultural critic, Patrick Chamoiseau (2018: 73), who argues that we need to go beyond hierarchical or patronizing solutions for the displaced. He is insistent that the normal acceptance of asymmetry and difference between the powerful and the powerless needs to be disrupted and transcended. Chamoiseau (2018: 75) continues:

> Welcoming migrants, who come who go who stay who continue on, welcoming them without demands, is to honour a future within them. To trust them with their own future. Relation

assigns no fixity, semblance or resemblance, no intangible, and therefore fictive difference. No obligatory ancestor. It makes do with separations, distortion, or fertile divergences. It does not fear the unforeseeable. Relation is what instils in multiculturalism, the 'trans-' of open living together.

Chamoiseau does not specify where these open, shared spaces emerge. This is where we can insert some spatial awareness and specificity, identifying three modes of shared space:

- First, the shared space in relatively autonomous refugiums, where displaced people are gathered by necessity or choice. Here, Relation, used in Glissant's sense, defines the first stage of identity-making, where those of different heritage identities will have to learn to live together
- Second, the shared space between refugiums in the expansive archipelago called Refugia, where Refugians-at-large will have to work together to maximize their bargaining power with nation-states and international organizations. This shared space will broaden as Refugia enhances mobility across the archipelago and fosters both the conventional and creative economies
- Third, we need to adumbrate the shared spaces between refugiums and their surrounding countries (Somewherelands). We have adopted the expression 'social ecotones' to describe these contact zones and communal spaces. This idea requires a separate explication.

'Ecotones' have hitherto been used in biology to refer to the meeting points between two (or more) biomes. In defining how the idea can become sociological as well as botanical, two innovative scholars have argued that 'an ecotone may also indicate a place where two communities meet, at times creolizing or germinating into a new community' (Misrahi-Barak and Lacroix 2019). While social ecotones remain underdeveloped theoretically, we can see how they might work. In complete contrast to a 'no man's land', which is left deliberately empty due to mutual fear and suspicion, an ecotone would be both deliberately and spontaneously filled by those who seek a more profound cultural and social fusion, a deep Relational process also known as creolization (Cohen 2007). Those who want to retain their own identities could remain outside the social ecotones, while those who want to explore and modify their liquid social identities could step forward into ecotonic space.

We can illustrate this idea in praxis. An advocacy group called 'Otra Nation' has developed an illustrative proposal in response to President Trump's open competition to design his wretched 'wall' between Mexico and the USA. Completely subverting his plan, Otra Nation suggested that rather than a wall of separation, the countries separated by boundaries should 'bridge nations by creating communities based on shared principles of economic resiliency, energy interdependence and a trust-based society'. In particular, Otra Nation will be a 'shared co-nation open to citizens of both Mexico and the United States and co-maintained by [their] respective governments. Physical land and the initial investment will be provided by both countries, and the infrastructure and services will be built with a workforce of 50 per cent Mexican and 50 per cent American. Otra Nation will be the world's first continental bi-national socio-ecotone' (Sinclair 2018). Needless to say, Otra Nation did not win Trump's competition.

The commons and 'mobile commons'

Historically, 'the commons' alludes to certain goods – air, water, the oceans – that have always been associated with common use, rather than private ownership. The word 'commons' also evokes and honours those who still support the old forms of communalism and usufruct, who tenaciously insist that not every village square, island, forest, park, pond, mountain, or glacier has to be handed over to the property developers. (By way of illustration, some 1.5 million hectares, or one-twentieth of the land in Britain and Ireland, are still classified as common land.)

While overuse and selfish behaviour have sometimes spoiled commonly held resources – this is known as 'the tragedy of the commons' – there are also many examples of communities successfully and far-sightedly sharing the commons. Elinor Ostrom's (1990) pioneering work, for which she won the Nobel Prize, proposed eight design principles for the successful collective management of natural resources. These have been picked over theoretically and robustly tested in 91 studies. As a result of this scrutiny, Cox et al. (2010) have produced a modified list of principles for a successful commons, which, in summary, are: (a) defining boundaries between legitimate users and non-users, (b) congruence with local social and environmental conditions, (c) matching input and appropriation, (d) participation in making the rules, (e) monitoring the rules and the resources of the community, (f) graduated sanctions for those who break the rules, (g) conflict-resolution mechanisms, (h) the right to organize, and (i) appropriate 'nesting' of different activities and enterprises.

Without having to interrogate these principles in detail, we can confidently say that governance of commonly held resources *can* work without the iron hand of state bureaucracies or the heavy-handed instructions of national politicians. There is, however, one important difference between historical examples of the management of the commons and the situation facing contemporary displacees. In the first instance, habitual practices generated over generations validate communal social practices. The new commons are made on the move as refugees are dispersed, formed, reformed, and co-operatively engage with longer-established residents in the spaces in which they find themselves. Papadopoulos and Tsianos (2013: 190–1) suggest that such practices can be usefully described as a 'mobile commons'. In developing this idea, they argue that:

> People on the move create a world of knowledge, of information, of tricks for survival, of mutual care, of social relations, of services exchange, of solidarity and sociability that can be shared, used and where people contribute to sustain and expand it.... The mobile commons is neither private nor public, neither state owned nor part of civil society; rather it exists to the extent that people share it and generate it as they are mobile and when they arrive somewhere.

They suggest that the mobile commons comprises five elements: (a) a shared knowledge of routes, shelter, local economies, social support, and surveillance, (b) ways of distributing this knowledge including social networks and social media, (c) the self-generated means of delivering goods and services, (d) links to civil society organizations, social movements, and campaigns, and (e) mutual support, exchange, and friendship, including some forms of transnational co-operation (Papadopoulos and Tsianos 2013: 191–2).

Homemaking on the move: A gendered approach

The creation of a mobile commons logically debouches into the need for people who have no homes to engage in homemaking. Whether for private or communal use, new homes have to be built by people who have failed to find a permanent place 'to hang their hats'. Homemaking on the move is not a normal situation, but we can think of a few precedents and examples. Visualize, for example, the Mongolian nomads-of-old fashioning their dwellings (yurts) from latticework and skins, as they followed their herds around the Eurasian steppes. Contrast that romantic image of constructing and reconstructing homes with the Rohingya of 2018, desperately throwing up shelters of bamboo and tarpaulins, as they fled Myanmar for Bangladesh. For many displacees, the reality of shelter is not a close-to-nature nomadic lifestyle or a habitual commons. If they are lucky, they might gain access to UNHCR-supplied tents. For many Rohingya, a worse outcome awaited. They scrabbled around with local materials trying to make or enhance temporary lean-tos, with the aid of sympathizers and non-governmental organizations (NGOs). The degradation of their former houses denotes a material, social, and, not least, an emotional loss. Likewise, as Tolia-Kelly (2018) contends, Syrian displacees live in a state of precarity, their former homes, genealogies, cultural practices, landscapes, and heritages having been erased through bombing and forced migration.

Even where displacees have washed up in one place for years, homemaking has taken a provisional form. The abrupt rupture with their former lives, the lack of recognition of their human rights and emotional needs, their lack of legal status, and their limited access to goods and services, have arrested or delayed the normal processes of homemaking. There are particular aspects of homemaking on the move that are gendered and also impact differently on children.

In strongly patriarchal and religious societies, household spaces are often highly segregated. While it is often the case that the bedroom and the kitchen are oppressive spaces where domesticity and separation are enforced, they are also sites where, for at least part of the day, privacy and female solidarity can be stimulated. All this is challenged in the grim conditions of many refugee settlements. Tents can be slashed, while flimsy carpets and wall hangings can be pulled aside exposing women to prying eyes and children to sexual abuse.

Brun and Fábos (2015) have developed a sophisticated feminist framework to understand home and homemaking in situations of protracted displacement. They distinguish home (lower case) as the day-to-day practices of homemaking, from Home (capital H) signifying the memories, values, and sentiments attached to a past home, and HOME (all capital letters), indicating the ways in which global inequalities and indignities frame any new meaning of home and its institutional setting. The last is perhaps the most difficult conceptually, but using this trichotomy confers great advantages, allowing us to understand the different aspects of homemaking. Although Brun and Fábos suggest that the different forms of homemaking take place synchronously, we add the thought that the dynamic of homemaking in Refugia might evolve over time in successive phases.

The construction of home in the complex sense just described means that we need to liberate the discussion from mere technical fixes (for example, replacing tents with flat-pack houses) and from the mere act of delivering immediate help to the vulnerable. The next aspect of Homemaking (with a capital H) involves recovering and, where emotionally necessary, erasing memories of past homes. This vital task often falls to women, who have to answer the insistent questions of children, like: 'What has happened to granny and grandpa'? 'Will I ever see my friend or my teacher again'? 'When will we go back to our house'? 'Why can't I go to school'? 'Why is daddy so sad'? On the reverse side of the coin, a piece of previous jewellery, a holy book, a favourite garment, or the redolent smells of cooking a familiar dish can allow the fragmentary and provisional reconstruction of a former life and offer an affective conduit to constructing a new life.

Providing a rudimentary shelter and recovering memories remain important tasks, but the politics of HOME (the third stage or aspect) involve a more fundamental political contest as displacees recognize that they will have to confront their misfortune by challenging the system that has placed them at the bottom of the heap. This is when the struggle for HOME involves an alternative political and social vision for the future, a more elemental struggle for human rights and dignity. As Tolia-Kelly (2018: 216) argues:

> For many transcultural communities barely surviving migration, there is huge challenge in being able to retain cultural identities, values and practices. A loss of connectedness, cultural space and identity is a human rights issue, and can lead to a large-scale problem of thousands of forcibly displaced peoples suffering anomie, alienation, isolation, and violent erasure of a possibility of a future for their language, genealogies and cultural practices and heritage. At the heart of human rights is a right to shelter, to a home. 'Home' is the very thing that defines the diasporic imagination; it shapes hope, loss, fear and identities.

The uses of utopian thinking

When some idea is described as 'utopian', the implication is that it is unattainable, or a figment of the imagination. Such disparagers see themselves as having their feet on the ground. They deal with reality, not fantasy. We reject this derogatory perspective. With some others, our understanding of utopianism is very different from the popular view. Indeed, we see utopianism as an essential component of human progress and a powerful means of reasoning.

The pursuit of socialism had become the main focus of utopian thinking for the last century, and with the collapse of nearly all Socialist experiments, utopian thinking went out of fashion. As a result, we have far too few utopias just when we need them most. Fortunately, utopian thinking is slowly reviving in recent years in dedicated research clusters like the Ralahine Centre for Utopian Studies and through the work of individual scholars.[1] In his bid to disarm those who dismissed utopian thinking as far-fetched or whimsical, the utopian thinker Ernst Bloch talked of 'concrete utopias'. Similarly, the American political philosopher John Rawls used the expression 'realistic utopias', while we have adopted the idea of 'pragmatic utopias', widely used in architecture and planning. Perhaps these adjectival qualifications to the word utopia concede too much, as utopian thinking is more real, concrete, and pragmatic than is conventionally assumed. Indeed, the argument can be turned on its head. As Levitas (2013: xii) reasons, 'for those who still think that utopia is about the impossible, what really is impossible is to carry on as we are, with social and economic systems that enrich a few but destroy the environment and impoverish most of the world's population'. To this, we will add that in the arena of migration, what is impossible is to accept a situation where millions of people flee for their lives and languish in despair without trying to envisage a radical alternative.

Again, with Levitas (2013: 218), we see 'utopia as method' that allows us to build alternative scenarios in a rich and inventive way: like her, our intention is 'to make explicit a method that is already in use wherever and whenever people individually or collectively consider what the future might bring and how human might chose to shape it'. In other words, utopian thinking transforms ideas about what is, to what could be, and then what should be.

Conclusion

In trying to convey the idea of Refugia, we have found ourselves having to tackle a number of taken-for-granted preconceptions, which, in this chapter, we have sought to challenge. A political world simply comprising nation-states is an orthodoxy reinforced by everything from passports to sporting competitions, trade statistics, political commentaries, and journalistic discourses. But the organization of political and economic power is, in practice, much more varied and, we suggest, can readily accommodate a new, if unusual, political arrangement like Refugia. Besides, further territorial expressions of national identities are increasingly unviable.

Although this is more readily acknowledged, in like manner, social identities have now escaped the cage of national identities. The idea that there are multiple, complex, overlapping, and situationally specific identities has moved from the recherché sphere of social theory to everyday encounters, often described as 'identity politics'.

We emphasize that social identities are less and less a zero-sum game, requiring participants to give up one in favour of another. Thus, it is perfectly possible (in our proposal) for individuals, families, and wider groups to declare themselves to be Refugians, while also retaining their diasporic roots or aspiring to integrate into an existing nation-state.

More unusual is our advocacy of archipelagic and ecotonic thinking. The first notion can be compared with the islands that make up an archipelago, the pearls that make up a necklace, or the stars that make up a constellation. These analogies are helpful in making evident that the components are intrinsically linked to the whole, but − this is where we need to modify the exact analogy − they are continuously and repeatedly reconfigured and reconnected (in Relation, as Glissant puts it). When this happens, the *oikos*, signifying a grim everyday confined reality, can morph into a new kind of *polis*. Again, to echo John Donne's famous poem, each refugium is not an island entire of itself, but is surrounded by and imbricated with other refugiums in increasingly networked similar places. Their mutual, intertwined connections, their ecotones, together with the homes they fashion creatively and communally, will determine the success of Refugia.

In each refugium (and later and dynamically across Refugia as a whole), multifarious and gendered processes of homemaking are undertaken to fashion shelters, recover, modify, or elide memories, and lastly, to effect more fundamental changes in the status of displacees. Because these processes of collective homemaking are made on the move, we have suggested that a modified notion of 'the commons', a 'mobile commons' provides a way of understanding how virtual, transitory, and more-anchored spaces are fashioned between the cracks of settled communities.

Finally, we argued that to construct Refugia, we need to escape the tethers of the 'real' and the 'acceptable', reject the dulling of the imagination, and embrace the human capacity to envisage an imaginative and original future. We favour bold utopian thinking, which shows us the world to which Refugians and those who support them can and should aspire, and the one which they can, brick by brick, build.

VIGNETTE (2029)

What shall we do with the Johnsons? Decision-time in the Refugium Tindouf (Registered No. 116/2024)

They were a rag-tag bunch. Some had crossed the English Channel in a flotilla of converted pleasure boats, dodged the French border guards, and made their way through France and Spain across the Mediterranean to North Africa. There they had merged with others who had quit Spain after their pensions had plummeted in value and desperate attempts to refinance their apartments went belly up. There was not much love lost between them. Nevertheless, a caravan of ageing combusti-motors had made their way to Tindouf in the Sahara where they heard there was a community of refugees.

So there was, but the Tindouf Refugians had already seen stories on their newsfeed of a group of dishevelled Brexitanians, popularly known as 'Johnsons' (no-one knew why), entering the Moroccan desert and coming their way. Their pink-red skins and split lips made them a sorry sight: the desert crossing had taken its toll.

They hoped to find shelter in Tindouf, where they might be able to make a life, and maybe send a bit of money to their impoverished relatives back in bankrupt Brexitania. Or, once in the refugium, perhaps they could move on to some other part of Refugia and rebuild their lives. For now, though, they were stuck.

Most of the people in the Tindouf Refugium were refugees from the Sahel wars, and they met in the agora to decide the Johnsons' fate. Would these white English fit in if they were admitted? Race shouldn't be a factor. But weren't they economic migrants rather than refugees anyway? Not that Refugia was all that hot on that distinction. Most Refugians and Solidarians were sympathetic to the Johnsons' plight, but some recalled how Brexitania had almost completely shut its borders in the first part of the 2020s, admitting hardly anyone but the rich.

To be fair, these Johnsons should not be blamed for the actions of their government, should they? More troubling were the rumours of Identitarian sympathizers among them, and even Disrupters prepared to use violence. While confidence in the refugium and in Refugia more widely was sturdy enough, the assembly thought they could do without this kind of challenge.

The decision was close, but there was a clear majority (52–48 per cent). The Johnsons would be given 'temporary leave to remain' for three months, then asked to move on.

Note

1 For the Ralahine Centre see Higgins (2012). Perhaps the most highly regarded utopian thinker of the twentieth century is the philosopher, Ernst Bloch. The reprinting of his three-volume account called *The principle of hope* (1995), first published in German over the period 1954–1959, and his book, *The spirit of utopia* (2000), first published in German in 1918, testify to the revival and enduring appeal of utopian thought.

3

ALTERNATIVE VISIONS

From an arc to 'Zatopia'

We are not, of course, the only scholars, policymakers, activists, and observers who have noticed that the current refugee regime is fracturing, if not completely broken. In this chapter, we will appraise the views of critics emanating from within the community of refugee scholars and who are similarly despairing of the long-held solutions to mass displacement. These 'insiders' have offered alternative ideas to some degree compatible with our proposal, though they still remain (in our view) somewhat within the realm of the orthodox. We turn next to more unconventional interventions – starting with a Californian-based real estate investor who proposed what he calls a 'refugee nation'. We discuss proposals to build 'refugee islands', including a plan developed by a respected Dutch architect. Other commentators and activists see potential in sanctuary and welcoming cities, developing 'incubator villages', refugee cities, or creating a structure called 'Zatopia'. In all cases, we adopt a stance of critical engagement, recognizing the proposals we consider here as constructive, worthy, and sometimes passionate attempts to grapple with a crisis that collectively we are all trying to solve.

Insider critiques: An arc of protection

Among the most important internal critical voices is that of T. Alexander Aleinikoff, who is currently the director of the Zolberg Institute on Migration and Mobility at the New School in New York, but served for five years, from 2010 to 2015, as deputy high commissioner in the Office of the United Nations High Commission for Refugees. He sets out his case in a series of interventions brought together in an e-book, co-authored with Leah Zamore, titled *The Arc of Protection* (2018). Their diagnosis of the challenge (Aleinikoff and Zamore 2018: 2) is acute and to the point:

> A humanitarian system established to provide emergency care is now called upon to render services for long and indefinite periods of time. Perhaps most fundamentally, no formal process or dependable practice of international responsibility-sharing – vital to finding solutions for refugee situations and to ensuring the dignified and lawful treatment of refugees in the interim – currently exists. The result is that millions of refugees around the world experience a second exile – years spent in limbo with little opportunity to rebuild their lives or contribute to the communities that host them. Most spend those years struggling to survive in just a handful of developing countries. *The refugee crisis is not global; but the crisis of responsibility is* [our emphasis].

Against this background, they suggest five principles of protection for uprooted people. The first three are derived from the original premises of the refugee regime: the provision of *safety* for those fleeing harm; the *enjoyment of asylum* to enable people to rebuild their lives; and the development of *solutions* by helping them to cease being uprooted altogether. They add two other principles, which resonate with the case that we present in this book. The first is to enhance opportunities for economic, educational, and social advancement through the possibility of *mobility*; and the second is for the displaced to have a role in crafting solutions to their displacement – in other words *voice* (Aleinikoff and Zamore 2018: 4). The focus on mobility and voice echoes to a considerable degree our starting point in this book.

As Aleinikoff and Zamore (2018: 1) put it, the inability of the displaced to find safety 'follows from the fact that states have collectively claimed the globe; there is no open, habitable space to which one can flee. So refugees are a "problem" that the international community of states both creates and must deal with; they must be let in somewhere. But where?'

The 'where' problem is one of the challenges we address with our proposal. But let us initially turn back to Aleinikoff and Zamore. Their solution is a disarmingly simple one: 'Let refugees move to where they can best rebuild their lives' (2018: 6). However, this movement is later qualified as 'movement within the regime' – that is, among those states that sign up to an enhanced international system of protection. Their proposal invokes the principle of the Nansen passport adopted in the first part of the twentieth century, which facilitated travel outside the state of asylum among those states that opted to recognize the document. Aleinikoff and Zamore (2018: 6–7) summarize the underlying logic of the Nansen passport like this: 'Refugees should be able to move among the members of the regime to find decent work, re-join family, access necessary health care, or pursue educational opportunities'.

Enhanced mobility would benefit all parties to the regime, these authors argue. Refugees would regain agency and self-reliance, host states would benefit if refugees unable to find employment could find it in another state, while destination states would gain from matching refugee workers to employers seeking labour. Smuggling would be undercut, deaths en route would decline, and the likelihood of exploitation would be reduced.

Aleinikoff and Zamore's proposals echo discussions in the late 1990s about responsibility-sharing (Hathaway and Neve 1997, Schuck 1997, Suhrke 1998). In diverse ways, these analysts explored collective solutions and regional approaches, recognizing that states might contribute in different ways. For example, Hathaway and Neve (1997: 190) suggested that solutions to displacement might be 'implemented by groups of states that feel that common interests, albeit varying in degree and impact, merit a shared response'. They called these 'interest convergence groups' and suggested that 'overall participation and net protection resources will be maximized by allowing states to make varying kinds of commitment to an interest convergence group'.

Such groups would often be neighbours geographically, but not necessarily so: some more distant territories might see it as in their interest to participate. Hathaway and Ghezelbash (2018) have recently revisited this idea in the Asia-Pacific context, arguing that responsibility for providing protection to refugees should shift from the national to the regional level. The basic premise would be that asylum seekers could apply for protection anywhere in the stated region.

There are elements in these past and current proposals – notably pertaining to mobility and to cross nation-state initiatives – that chime with our ideas in this book. But they are flawed by two major limitations. First, all of the authors so far discussed remain locked in their acceptance of the nation-state system, a taken-for-granted world view that we sought to challenge in Chapter 2. Second, they have an expectation that states will do the right thing, which has regrettably not been borne out over the last two decades and currently seems even less likely to gain traction. This faith in nation-states to act generously is surprising, as Aleinikoff (2017a) himself noted at a presentation at the University of California, because the failing refugee regime was put together *for* states *by* states, states are the problem, and thus cannot fix it. Regionalization (so-called 'burden sharing') may of course help particular states, but we strongly maintain that a more fundamental alternative to the administration of the refugee regime by the nation-state system is required.

To move to a more positive note, separately, and in association with Zamore, Aleinikoff makes three further crucial interventions with which we concur. He:

- Insists on giving refugees' *voice* and *agency* (though agency runs a poor second-place in his narrative)
- Recognizes the emergence of a transnational consciousness among refugees
- Sees the potential of linking digital technology to refugee representation.

Aleinikoff (2017b: 548) cogently argued these last two points when he suggested that 'through new technology and new media, refugees are beginning to foster new forms of community'. He advances the idea that, through increased connectivity, refugees can form transnational virtual communities: 'these communities – like all communities – serve a variety of functions: providing members with news from home, creating a space for political discussions (a space that may not have existed in the home country), maintaining cultural links (holidays, stories, recipes, music)'. From our point of view, this is a case of 'so near and yet so far'. By all means, have discussions and exchange recipes and stories – these will provide the cultural undergirding to a shared identity – but we need also to add virtual voting, assemblies, lobbying, legislation, collecting and distributing tax revenues, constitution-making, digital work, virtual courts, and a multitude of other online functions that can go into the making of our transnational polity, Refugia, and are discussed elsewhere in this book.

Insider critiques: Integration and incubation

Perhaps the most widely discussed recent attempt to rethink and trans-form the 'broken refugee system' is that undertaken by Betts and Collier (2017). Both are insiders to the world of refugee research and policy. Alexander Betts is professor of forced migration and international affairs, while Paul Collier has written on migration matters within his broader remit as professor of economics and public policy. (Like us, both are at Oxford University, though our common institutional affili-ation has not influenced our views.) At the core of their approach is the establishment of 'safe havens' in the countries in the developing world that neighbour conflict and crisis (Betts and Collier 2017).

Unfortunately, the expression 'safe haven' sends a chill down the spines of those concerned with refugee protection, as it recalls the 8000 Bosniak men and boys killed in the UN-designated 'safe area' of Srebrenica in 1995 by units of the Serb army. Even the 'good guys', the Dutch soldiers, who were meant to protect refugees, were drawn into this horror story. In 2014, the Dutch Supreme Court found the Dutch government responsible for the deaths of 300 refugees under its care. The evocation of 'safe havens' probably still fuels some redolent anxieties stemming from Srebrenica, but we concur with Betts and Collier, that any solution undoubtedly must start with where most refugees are. We agree too, that if it proves possible for displacees to remain in their (broadly defined) 'origin regions', it is more likely that they can return and rebuild their communities. Thus, allocating scarce resources to such regions may be more efficient and sustainable than other approaches. Within such regions, Betts and Collier reason, 'development areas' could be developed in the peripheral and border locations that often accommodate refugees. Instead of camp-based humanitarian assistance, which they say results in 'humanitarian silos', they place emphasis on autonomy and employment.

Two models for such development areas are suggested, which represent the ends of a spectrum of participation from 'integration' to 'incubation'. At the 'integration' end of the spectrum, exemplified partially by Uganda, where refugees are able legally to work, refugees gradually secure socio-economic and political rights alongside host citizens. The authors show how Uganda has taken a more liberal approach to refugees than many other hosting countries. For several decades, it has allowed refugees access to land, markets, and employment, and permitted them to start up businesses. As a result, refugees in long-running refugee settlements like Nakivale, as well as those who take their chances in cities like the capital Kampala, are able at least to survive, and sometimes thrive, they claim. Such an economically liberal model seems to work reasonably well in this setting, Betts and Collier aver.[1]

At the 'incubation' pole, partly exemplified by Jordan, particular spaces may be delineated where livelihoods can be pursued: a rather more segregated approach than in the Ugandan case. Refugees in Jordan – many of them Syrians – are far more circumscribed than in Uganda, but, according to Betts and Collier, there are still possibilities for livelihood here too. They alight on the example of the King Hussein bin Talal Development Zone, a Special Economic Zone (SEZ) in Jordan not far from the Zaatari refugee camp, contending that it would make sense to bring together the underutilized labour in the camp and the labour-short commercial and industrial plant in the SEZ for mutual benefit. They acknowledge that employers in SEZs have a bad reputation for the exploitation of workers, but suggest that this need not necessarily be the case. Among other things, the experience could 'incubate' portable skills and businesses that could be transferred home if conflict abates (Betts and Collier 2017). Betts and Collier submit that different approaches will be more feasible and desirable according to context, and, by further extending the notion of incubation, argue that variants along this spectrum of approaches can in time stimulate recovery and return after conflict ends.

Other insiders have proposed similar ideas. Kilian Kleinschmidt, a former UNHCR official who served as senior field coordinator at the Zaatari camp, suggests that such 'cities of tomorrow' could include Special Development Zones, 'designated areas with special administrative frameworks, policies, and services designed to produce inclusive economic development'. Such zones would offer protection and assistance, including social services for refugees and other migrants and would 'leverage mass displacement for the benefit of the local population by encouraging entrepreneurship, self-sufficiency, and new investment in jobs and infrastructure' (Kleinschmidt 2019).

Much of this approach is not new: indeed 'refugee self-reliance', 'refugees as development assets', and kindred perspectives have long become part of mainstream ideas on resolving displacement (Crisp 2001). In this sense, the Betts and Collier approach represents a well-argued repackaging of established 'insider' perspectives. Again, we have to evoke some problems with their analysis. In their illustrations, the goodwill of nation-states is necessary (Uganda in the first case, Jordan in the second), though there is a welcome recognition of mutual interest rather than the more naïve conventional narrative of generosity. We would like more emphasis on refugee agency and the internal building of political structures, though the occasional elicitation of 'autonomy' is helpful and converges with our view. Finally, for us, the prescription offered is rather too neo-liberal. Refugees appear predominantly as proto-proletarians or proto-entrepreneurs, useful for their labour or their enterprise – perhaps a rather limited view of their potential. (Cannot refugees also be poets, dancers, musicians, teachers, politicians, or researchers?) Despite these reservations, we acknowledge Betts and Collier's determination to address the big picture, which resonates with the approach we have taken in this book.

Unconventional interventions: A refugee nation

Because observers can often see more of the game than the players, it may be helpful to give serious consideration to interventions outside the circle of refugee policymakers and scholars. One such intervention was made by Jason Buzi, an entrepreneur resident in California. The idea of creating or promoting a separate 'refugee nation' was first promoted by Buzi on a dedicated web site, with a more detailed proposal available as an e-pamphlet (Buzi 2015). His analysis of the scope of the refugee problem and the need for an urgent solution is similar to our views. He adds a number of remarks about how displaced people are 'forced to live in poverty', how they 'fall victim to traffickers', how older men prey on child brides, and how educated and trained refugees 'waste away' without using their skills. Buzi is particularly acute in seeing that external assistance, however expert or well intended, cannot match the potential for mobilizing displaced people themselves. He then abandons refugee agency to make an over-simplistic leap of logic: 'the solution is simple: for the millions of stateless people around the world – a state of their own'. This prescription contains one crucial elision – 58 per cent (40 million of the 68.5 million displacees in 2017) were internally displaced people, not therefore stateless. Although Buzi recognizes internally displaced people later in his argument, another telling problem is his continuous ambiguity, not to say confusion, between 'state' and 'nation' and between refugees who have crossed a national border (and who are therefore entitled under the 1951 Convention to protection by signatory governments) and those who have not.

One attractive element in Buzi's proposal – stemming, as he avows, from his real estate background – is that he directly addresses the issue of location. Where, he asks, is such a refugee nation or refugee state to be located? He answers that there are many inhabitable areas of the globe that are lightly populated and wonders whether one country could 'carve off a sparsely inhabited area'. Could some of the many uninhabited islands in the world be used? Could an existing sovereign state allow itself, with the approval of the population, to be taken over? Finally, he surmises, could a new island be built? (See below for a discussion of this idea from another source.) Examining the possibilities posed by Buzi is important precisely because any of these solutions present thorny political obstacles for existing states. In particular, the surrender of a significant mass of territory and a portion of sovereignty is unlikely to be a popular political option, despite Buzi's casual allusions to Indonesia's 17,000, and Micronesia's 600, uninhabited islands.

Because we ourselves deploy utopian thinking as a method, immediate political obstacles do not in themselves negate Buzi's speculative locations. However, he misses some more fundamental objections. Organizing and transporting very large numbers of people far from their home regions is an ethically dubious project, evoking the slave trade, indentured labour, or the transportation of convicts. The issue of consent and the garnering and mobilization of refugees' own ideas, preferences, and plans simply do not feature. Instead, the *dei ex machina* are largely derived from the foundational principles and conventional wisdoms prevalent in Buzi's adopted country, the US. True, he mentions NGOs and the UN, even a world government – but, practically speaking, he wishes to recruit to his cause such players as 'influential celebrities', 'super-rich individuals', investors, and those buying bonds in the enterprise. This US-centric vision is reinforced by his notion of the *desiderata* of his refugee nation – a 'robust constitution', free speech, freedom of religion, the separation of church and state, a 'robust (again) work culture', and a preference for a democratic, plural, capitalist society ('the most successful over the long-term').

We have no objection to the creation of a new 'refugee nation'. But because Buzi is unsure whether he is talking of a 'state' or a 'nation', he fails to make an intellectual break with the Westphalian system, whereby only territorially based nation-states comprise the units of international affairs. He relies far too much on the intervention of wealthy benefactors and investors and too little on refugees' views. He has not thought enough about the ethical dimensions of his proposals. Buzi predominately derives his model from the US, and he does not give sufficient space to self-organization and self-chosen constitutional preferences. Even when he departs from the US-inspired narrative, he does so ill-advisedly, alluding to Israel, his place of birth, as the paradigmatic refugee nation. The self-evident objection is that even if Israel provided a place of safety for distressed Jews, it created another disastrous refugee problem in the form of stateless Palestinians. Creating one nation-state only to generate further displacements from the territory in which it is established cannot be part of a general solution.

Refugee islands

It is remarkable how often islands appear in imagined solutions to the problem of mass displacement. Their popularity plays into a romantic view of island societies that is deeply embedded in Western cultures. Islands provide a good deal of imagery for poetry and fiction and for scientific and social comment. They represent an alternative vision to a developed Western industrial culture – one that is, in contrast, marked by a simple exchange economy, naturalness, an instinctive division of labour, and nostalgia for a pre-Industrial Age (Cohen 2017: 156–7). The 'state of nature' imagined by political philosophers was based on islands and, of course, More's *Utopia* (2016/1516) was an island. Islands are also places of isolation, insulation, and containment, and easy to define territorially.

With respect to playing a role in the crisis of displacement, as we have mentioned, islands appear in Buzi's 'refugee nation' where he refers to the many uninhabited islands in the Philippines and Indonesia. However, in September 2015, these vague suggestions were given dramatic impetus, accompanied by considerable media coverage, when Egyptian telecom billionaire Naguib Sawiris offered to buy an island to provide shelter for refugees facing death in crossing the Mediterranean. He announced his offer on Twitter: 'Greece or Italy sell me an island, I'll call it "independence" and host the migrants and provide jobs for them building their new country'. He later explained his ideas in an interview: 'You have dozens of islands which are deserted and could accommodate hundreds of thousands of refugees'. He thought the cost would be between US$10 million and US$100 million, but the main expense would be in providing infrastructure including temporary shelters, housing, schools, universities, and hospitals. He was aware of issues of jurisdiction and customs (Daily News and Analysis 2015). Although this offer seemed to come out of nowhere, his family is experienced at property development, though one wonders how much building 'temporary shelters' compares with the luxurious El Gouna resort on the Red Sea, which his brother Samih Sawiris had developed from its origins as a small village. In any event, Naguib Sawiris's plan cut no ice with Greek Prime Minister Alexis Tsipras, who gave him an audience, then ignored his offer to house 100,000 Syrian refugees on ten Greek islands. The UNHCR reacted to the proposal with similar disdain. 'What can I do? My conscience is clear that at least I tried', he lamented (MacBride 2016).

The most elaborately formulated island solution for refugees is to create a 'Europe-in-Africa' city-state on the Tunisian Plateau – a thin strip of seabed in the Mediterranean between Tunisia and Italy. According to this plan, which it is hoped the European Union would fund, the level of the seabed would be lifted, and the resultant land rented from Tunisia and Italy on a 99-year lease, thereby creating a new country, with its own passport, constitution, economy, and social system. The concept has been modelled in detail by Theo Deutinger, a respected Dutch architect. The design will incorporate elements from Europe and Africa: a mosque like in Casablanca, a church like St Peter's in Rome, a university like Oxford, an urban fabric like in Timbuktu, and so on. Initially Europe-in-Africa would cater for 150,000 people, but it can be expanded by pouring more sand onto the shallow shelving (Taylor 2016).

The island solutions proposed by Buzi, Sawiris, and Deutinger are, we suggest, inventive constructions that are worthy of some consideration and, in Deutinger's case, may provide a way through the unhelpful conflation of sovereignty and territory. Buzi and Sawaris made no challenge to this coupling, simply assuming that they would have to accept the authority of the governments of the Philippines, Indonesia, Greece, or Italy. Deutinger's idea of purchasing a 99-year lease from adjacent countries is more promising, especially since we can envisage a legal personality, Refugia, that could sign such a lease, perhaps with the option of buying a freehold at the end of the period. Of course, there are other objections to an island solution. Unless we are thinking of scores of islands, the scale is too small to address the magnitude of the refugee population, especially since creating an island from scratch is expensive and time consuming. Such a scheme also risks disrupting the delicate marine environment of shallow waters. The lavishly engineered three artificial islands off Dubai present just such a dismal warning. Coastal erosion, threats to marine fauna, and changes in wave patterns have made that experiment at upscale living a frequent target of environmental groups like Greenpeace.

Island solutions bear some resemblance to the kind of enclaves that some have proposed next to existing settlements, in a sort of benign separation or segregation. For example, Menasse and Guérot (2016) suggest, 'We don't need to rub up against each other and rub each other up the wrong way. In short: we don't need *integration*. We respect "*otherness*" – and we let the new arrivals be in their "otherness"'. They propose that refugees in Europe could be allocated land next to European cities, which would create space for modes of living along-side already existing settlements: 'In this way, New Damascus and New Aleppo, New Madaya and so on could arise in the middle of Europe. Or New Diyarbakir or New Erbil and New Dohuk for the Kurdish refugees. Perhaps also New Kandahar or New Kunduz for the Afghan refugees'. After being provided with basic site and services infrastruc-ture, the new arrivals would look after themselves, in line with their culture, cuisine, music, and social structures. This would allow 'prox-imity with respect, *an alliance of alterity* under the same European law, a creative network of diversity' (Menasse and Guérot 2016). Over time, residents of neighbouring towns would mix, and eventually only the 'New' in the place name would remind people that the town's founders came from elsewhere. There are some elements of interest here, but the ethnic exclusivity implied by this proposal jars with the more inclusive aspirations of ours.

Sanctuary and welcoming cities

'Sanctuary' has a complex history, referring in the classical world to sacred spaces like shrines shielded from outsiders. It was used also in the Christian tradition to refer to churches where runaway slaves or even criminals could be given protection from state authorities. The crucial shift in usage is that nowadays city mayors and local councillors (particularly in the US, United Kingdom, and Canada) have responded to humanitarian concerns by turning their localities into 'sanctuary cities' offering protection for international refugees. This has given rise to a profound discursive and political challenge to national governments. As Bauder (2017: 182) notes, providing local identification documents (IDs) or recognizing foreign IDs contests the idea of an exclusive national sovereignty and 'rearticulates who belongs in the community and who does not', thus crucially shifting 'the scale of belonging from the national to the local'.[2]

As the movement behind sanctuary spread to many cities in California, confrontation with President Trump became inevitable. In characteristic mode, he opined that 'the state of California's attempts to nullify federal law have sparked a rebellion by patriotic citizens who want their families protected and their borders secured', reserving a special blast for the mayor of Oakland, California who, he thought, should be prosecuted for warning residents of an imminent operation by the immigration agency (*Guardian*, 16 May 2018).

Encouragingly, an increasing number of city officials are intervening at national and international levels to help shape policies concerning migration and displacement. As Muggah and Sikorski (2018) note, the crucial intercession came in 2017, when the International Organization for Migration, together with the United Cities and Local Government, gathered together 150 cities to sign the seven-page Mechelen Declaration (2017), which, inter alia, committed the cities to

> strengthen cooperation among local and regional governments, particularly to replicate successful practices in city-to-city cooperation on migration issues, including across borders, and also commit to strengthening other partnerships, including those with intergovernmental agencies, the private sector, and migrant and diaspora associations. ... We commit to work with States to fulfil at the local level their international commitments to ensure full respect for the human rights of refugees, internally displaced persons and migrants, regardless of their migratory status, and that of child-oriented policies, where necessary.

Among other initiatives, Muggah and Sikorski (2018) list the following developments:

- More than 100 cities in the US have declared themselves as 'welcoming cities', promoting integration and inclusion for refugees
- Some 500 jurisdictions in the US describe themselves as 'sanctuary cities', despite threats to cut their federal funding if they persist in their efforts to support refugees

- In the UK, there are some 80 'cities of sanctuary' offering help to refugees
- Other city forums that have addressed refugee issues include the Global Parliament of Mayors, the International Coalition of Inclusive and Sustainable Cities, and Urban 20, an initiative led by the mayors of Paris and Buenos Aires.

In the wake of the migration crisis of 2015–2016, many other cognate initiatives emerged in Europe, particular in the southern part of the region, where Greece, Italy, and Spain were at the forefront of large-scale arrivals of migrants. Again, these municipal initiatives were often at odds with the interests of national governments. A notable example is the case of 'Barcelona, Refuge City', whose progressive mayor, Ada Colau, welcomed refugees (albeit in relatively small numbers), against the wishes of the Spanish state (Barcelona City Council 2016; Colau 2015). The 'Barcelona, Refuge City' plan was launched in September 2015 in response to the migration crisis with the aim of gearing up the city to receiving and assisting refugees, providing the necessary services, guaranteeing their rights, and fostering participation in civil society. There was a significant transnational dimension to this work, both in practice and in statements of intent, pointing to the potential prefiguration of Refugia as a transnational entity. In mid-September 2015, Mayor Ada Colau and her colleagues launched their manifesto, 'We, the cities of Europe', which proclaimed:

> We, the cities of Europe, are ready to become places of refuge. We want to welcome these refugees. States grant asylum status, but cities provide shelter. Border towns, such as Lampedusa, or the islands of Kos and Lesbos, are the first to receive the flow of people seeking asylum, and European municipalities will have to take these people in and ensure they can start a new life, safe from the dangers from which they have escaped. We have the space, services and, most importantly, the support of our citizens to do so. Our municipal services are already working on refugee reception plans to ensure food, a roof, and dignity for everyone fleeing war and hunger. The only thing missing is state support. (Colau 2015)

In addition to Ada Colau, the manifesto was signed by Anne Hidalgo, mayor of Paris, and Spyros Galinos, mayor of Lesbos, and supported by a number of mayors elsewhere in Spain.

These city initiatives are far from perfect, nor without their critics, but on balance, they were positive moves that often contrasted with the stance of national governments and give grounds for thinking that these kinds of city initiatives may prefigure our vision of Refugia. As Bue Rübner Hansen, an academic and commentator on the transnational municipal initiatives, put it, 'Across Europe you see governments that are very reluctant to deal with this problem. The "refugee crisis" is a crisis of reception, of hospitality let's say, a crisis in the expectations we have of our governments to provide for people who are in dire need, and to guarantee their human rights' (Hansen and Thibos 2016). In contrast to governments, they argue, 'it is noticeable that many cities – and not just those who have the responsibility to deal with people when they arrive – are more willing to receive people in a decent way than their national governments' (ibid).

Refugees and asylum-seekers must treasure any friends they have and, of course, will be happy to find sanctuary and a welcome in some of the cities in which they find themselves. Yet, one cannot help wondering what the balance of power is between national policies of exclusion and local practices of inclusion. We have noted this contestation in the US, but perhaps nowhere has this tension been more evident than in Italy, where it has dramatically played out in the little Calabrian village of Riace. As in many European villages, the young had left, the school was about to close, and there were numerous empty properties. A visionary mayor, Domenico Lucano, had the idea of inviting refugees to revive the town, comprising 1800 locals. Ultimately 450 migrants and refugees came, from more than 20 countries. He gained worldwide attention as he unveiled, then rolled out, his innovative plan, which many thought it might be a model for rural Europe at large. As Mayor Lucano put it, 'There were people without a house here, and there were houses without people here. It's simple' (BBC News 2016).

In 2016, the mayor was listed by *Fortune* as one of the world's greatest leaders. He was hailed as a humanitarian champion, which, undoubtedly, he was. However, the plan was always crucially dependent on having continuing access to national funds for refugee reception and settlement. When a right-wing populist government of Italy was elected, the new Minister of the Interior, Matteo Salvini, lost little time in making his anger upfront and personal. Funds were cut, the mayor was placed under house arrest for alleged fraud and accused of arranging fraudulent marriages of convenience to allow migrants to stay in Italy. Salvini welcomed the news of the mayor's arrest by tweeting 'Let's see what all the other do-gooders who want to fill Italy with immigrants will say now' (Giuffrida 2018). It seems that, for the moment anyway, national pressures are winning, and the refugees are slowly leaving Riace.

Other proposals

Incubator villages

Although the word 'incubator' suggests a link to the proposal by Betts and Collier discussed above, we are referring here to the idea of 'incubator villages' advanced by Johannes Cornelis van Nieuwkerk (2018), a communications and management specialist with an interest in innovative ideas and intercultural engagement. His starting point is the observation that even after recognition and acceptance, it takes an average of five years to resettle refugees in a European host country or return them to their countries of origin. This period, he plausibly argues, can be used to create a phase of 'basic integration' (to be funded by the European Union) and to provide Internet-based education, language skills, and welfare needs. Because refugees can be housed in low-cost, rural incubator villages, skills training, which will benefit refugees in the long run, can be substituted for high subsistence costs in urban settings. van Nieuwkerk argues that existing villages will be revitalized, while 'final destination countries will receive tax-payers instead of welfare-recipients'.

Whereas the core idea of an incubator village is unobjectionable, van Nieuwkerk is disarmingly honest in confessing that his is a self-financed initiative that has so far failed to bring the relevant stakeholders together to operationalize a pilot project. As in some other proposals, his idea is one parachuted from above, rather than developed with, or by, refugees.

Refugee cities and better camps

A similarly top-down idea is to identify and legalize separate designated areas (sometimes called 'refugee cities' or a 'refuge city'), where
normal regulations governing refugee settlement need not apply.
This separate legal status makes the proposal distinct from the
existing cities designating themselves sanctuary or welcoming cities
(discussed earlier). In these new entities, refugees will be able to work
and to establish businesses. Instead of being dependent on aid, they
could establish viable micro-economies fuelled by internal growth
and external investments. This solution is similar to, or can usefully be linked to, Paul Romer's (2010) advocacy of 'charter cities'
as a means of fostering economic development in general. We have
not ourselves found Romer's own ideas particularly well-articulated
or tailored to the needs of refugees: his notion of 'charter cities' essentially addresses issues of the failing governance of certain urban areas.
However, Romer's status as a Nobel Laureate and chief economist
and senior vice president of the World Bank has lent considerable
authority to the notion. There are some serious attempts to apply
the idea of charter cities more specifically to the world of refugees,
the concept proposal on 'sustainable development zones' for refugees
being particularly notable (Rücker 2018). However, there is little in
the way of alternative world views – the dominance of conventional
neo-liberal economic thinking is evident in the proposals for refugee
cities we have found.

We conclude this section by referring briefly to two more ideas
for what we will call 'insulated societies'. The first is Bolleter and
Parish's (2019) Australian model for 'a bustling, multicultural and
entrepreneurial metropolis' to be located in the Northern Territory.
The idea has been generated in response to the increasing antagonism
of long-standing Australians to further immigration. The indebted-
ness to Romer's charter city is again evident, as is the normativity of
neo-liberal economics. More positively, the proposers suggest such a
city would provide refuge for many more migrants, over and above
Australia's humanitarian quota. The design has two unusual elements.
First, it is for car-phobic migrants (motorists will be excluded), and
second, refugees will be corralled in numerous ethnically defined

hexagonal spaces, 'homes away from home'. This mosaic of ethnic neighbourhoods will be linked by intersecting bus routes. We find ourselves making one familiar critique and another less so. A location is chosen for refugees, not by them. But perhaps rather more sinister is that cultural segmentation is assumed to be a natural good, as if refugees are incapable or unwilling ever to escape their heritage identities.

The second idea of an insulated society is not informed by utopian principles, but rather is predicated on realpolitik. Kaufmann (2018) asserts that as white majority populations will not accept large numbers of migrants from different ethnic and religious backgrounds, refugees will have to be accommodated somehow. His solution is building much more commodious, but decidedly closed, refugee camps, where they will be offered refuge, but not settlement. He allows that the newly encamped residents can travel to other camps or return to their home countries. But Kaufmann is primarily focused on damping down populism among the white majority populations, rather than the rights of refugees. No possibility of work, settlement, or political rights in nearby countries (we have called these Somewherelands) are allowed in Kaufmann's vision, and there is no focus on refugees' education, welfare, or development. For us, Refugia is a means of opening possibilities and enhancing mobilities, not walling people off.

Zatopia

Of all the alternative visions we have reviewed, we find Femke Halsema's plan for 'Zatopia' closest to ours in spirit, if not in detail. Halsema has a distinguished record of public service (she is currently Amsterdam's first female mayor), making a number of important political interventions across a number of fields.[3] For her and her colleagues in a small Dutch organization, 'Zatopia is a sanctuary between the boundaries of nation-states, a place where refugees find rights, security and a future even if they don't have residence of a country'.[4] She explicitly signals that hers is a vision of 'a utopian community', where refugees can take their fate into their own hands and govern themselves. There, refugees can work and study, build their own economy, maintain their schools, and manage their community.

While Halsema's proposals might sound fanciful, her intentions should be taken seriously. The predicate is that as refugees are not welcome, indeed as the doors of most nation-states remain shut, there is a need and a moral duty to create places where people can live their lives in safety and with dignity. These 'places' are not fully specified in the proposal. They seem to be both general and particular. The general is based on finding commons not under the control of the state or private property, while administering them on the sound principles established by the American political economists Elinor Ostrom (2016) and Wilson (2016b). (We have discussed Ostrom's principles in Chapter 2.) The particular is based on the site of the Zaatari refugee camp, on the border of Jordan and Syria, which looms large in a number of alternative visions. We assume that the name Zatopia is a portmanteau word combining Zaatari and utopia. (We discuss the Zaatari refugee camp in Chapter 4.)

We are reluctant to criticize an alternative proposal that is so close to ours in its basic diagnosis, that is, in the core understanding that there is a need to establish viable communities of refugees without the need to accept national citizenships or the discursive claim of nation-states to be the sole legitimate repositories of belonging and authority. Though there are some plans for phasing in Zatopia in various stages (from planning, to networking, and construction), it is difficult for us to discern progress, so perhaps the practical side of the proposal is not going anywhere fast. As we explain in Chapter 4, the Zaatari refugee camp is important, but is too frequently evoked as a paradigmatic case, rather than one with special characteristics. The connection between the various refugee communities (our refugiums) is also rather unambitious or lacks detail. (All that is said is 'the ultimate goal is the construction of one or more Zatopias'.) Nonetheless, we want to give our support to the advocates of Zatopia in their demands to force a public debate on refugees' access to public goods, to mobilize refugees as political subjects, to establish viable commons, and above all 'to break the paralysis in political and public debates'.

Conclusion

All the alternative visions we discuss display a mixture of reflection, passion, and engagement. They attest to our common humanity and the desperate need to find a solution for the problem of mass displacement. Of course, we do not cover every idea – indeed one of the difficulties in writing this book is that we found it impossible to respond to each suggestion or new lead supplied by our friendly readers or listeners. One reader asked, 'What about "seasteading"'? where communities are established on sea-based platforms. Well, not really – since the movement seems to be led by rich people trying to evade tax. 'What about communes and kibbutzim'? asked another. Clearly all communal experiments are relevant to our discussion, but we wanted to focus on those that were a direct response to the contemporary crisis in mass displacement. However, we are not mindless presentists and are, of course, open to further discussion of historical and comparative experiences.

If we were to identify some common threads in the proposals we *have* reviewed, there are clear distinctions between those made by insiders of the international refugee regimes, who having been involved practically, as office holders or as academic advisers, and those made by outsiders, commenting as concerned humanitarians. The former group are more inclined to chivvy agencies like the UNHCR and the International Organization for Migration into widening their briefs, to create regional solutions, and to recognize the role of market forces. They rarely question the legitimacy of the nation-state system, the role of the international agencies, or the hegemony of neo-liberal economics, all of which are taken as givens. The latter group, the outsiders, are more diverse in character and more inclined to blue-sky thinking. The group is varied, particularly in the matter of scale, with most thinking locally – for one a village, for others a modified camp, a refugee city, or a refugee island. Of course, there is an implicit assumption that their plans could be scaled up, but this is rarely spelled out. Only one or two of the outsiders are truly global in their remedies.

As authors of another vision, Refugia, we have learned a good deal from the alternative visions we have reviewed, but think there are some real imperatives that are sometimes missed:

- First, one needs to start with where refugees are – assuming they are transported here or there according to the caprice of the planner is neither practical nor ethical. Refugee agency begins with existing movements and the direction of movement
- Second, bold schemes are fine, but it would be helpful to any scheme if the proposer could demonstrate that there are existing prefigurations of her or his ideas (see Chapter 4, where we discuss this issue in the case of Refugia)
- Third, we think it is necessary to think beyond the current preoccupation with nation-states (who of course fund the international refugee regime) and to see the nation-state as part of the problem
- Fourth, similarly, many alternative visions have a remarkably narrow view of economics, rarely venturing beyond the neoclassical, even to Keynesian economics, let alone to the new economy movement (which centres on the health of people and the planet, not on Gross Domestic Product growth and bank balances)
- Fifth, a persistent lacuna is the failure to show how disparate refugee communities could connect with one another for mutual advantage (This is a vital aspect of Refugia.)
- Sixth, and finally, real engagement by refugees in any plan and a sense they are in charge will be necessary to its success. (We do not exempt ourselves from this criticism, though we have had some engagement on the ground, which has helped to shape our ideas.)

VIGNETTE (2029)

Serving time at the Brong Ahafo Refugium, Ghana (Registered No. 122/2024)

Lariba accelerated down the highway from Tamale in the solar en route to the assembly of the Brong Ahafo Refugium in Ejura. Slouched in the passenger seat was her friend Tekle, a Refugian originally from Eritrea, doing his time service in the Ghanaian refugium. He cranked up the volume of the Sai music blaring from the sound system.

Lariba tried to concentrate on her driving, while Tekle slumped further into the seat, his mind wandering. He ruefully reflected that national service, which had been compulsory in Eritrea, was the very reason he had to flee in the 2010s when he had first heard the music that was playing.

But time service in Refugia was a bit different – he felt that his efforts were contributing to something positive and bigger. And it was something that he *believed* in, instead of helping to prop up a corrupt regime. Time service in Refugia was nominally voluntary, but more or less expected. He was OK with that, and he liked the principle of Refugians working in refugiums other than their own. After all, his name meant 'to plant': wasn't that what he was doing in a way? The last time he served outside his home refugium in Somaliland was in the Rojava Refugium, helping the folks there cope with the Turkish military incursions that were still going on after all this time.

'Hey Fuj, turn that down a moment', said Lariba, interrupting his reverie. 'I can't hear myself think'.

He complied, and they snatched a bit of desultory conversation, switching between English and Fugee, the creole that was developing across Refugia. They couldn't always get their meanings across in Fugee – it was still an emerging language – so they often defaulted to English.

Lariba, a Ghanaian citizen and solidarian working in the refugium, told him how she did not resent the hassle of having to do a bit of time service, even though it was irritating, as it took her away from her young family. To be sure, Kwame would look after the kids. Men did more of that kind of stuff these days. Lariba liked to think that she helped to spread the principles of gender equality that Refugia promoted into the surrounding 'host' community. 'Social remittances', an assemblywoman had called it in an assembly meeting a while back. Lariba got the drift of that idea, but why did social stuff always get dressed up in economic language? Fuj!

Notes

1 The shine was taken off the story of Uganda's open-heartedness by the disclosure in October 2018 that the number of refugees hosted by the Ugandan government was 1.1 million rather than 1.4 million. Local officials had bumped up the figures to corruptly mismanage funds meant to support refugees (*Guardian*, 18 October 2018). Despite this depressing revelation, the Uganda experience is broadly a positive one.

2 This discursive rupture with the nation-state's proclaimed monopoly on belonging is, of course, entirely compatible with our proposal to use the *Sesame app/card/chip* as Refugia's form of ID, so an early task of the refugium assemblies will be to negotiate recognition of Refugians' residency and employment rights in sanctuary cities.

3 Before becoming mayor of Amsterdam, Femke Halsema was a member of the Dutch House of Representatives from 1998 to 2011. As her Wiki entry testifies, she has been a leading light in the 'green left' movement.

4 Quotations in this section are from the Dutch-language Zatopia website (Halsema 2016). Our apologies for any inadequacies in our translations of the Dutch originals. See also Halsema (2017).

4

REFUGIA NOW

Prefigurations

Of the various alternative visions reviewed in the previous chapter, some of the 'outsider' ideas, such as sanctuary/welcoming cities and Zatopia, resonate with our notion of Refugia and to some degree prefigure it – though we suggest that, among other differences, Refugia's transnational character distinguishes it from these proposals. In this chapter, we make the case that Refugia also exists in prefigured, albeit highly imperfect, form in the transnational practices of refugees and migrants that we can see all around us. We will first sketch the broad ways in which current transnational practices by refugees, migrants, and supportive citizens could be said to prefigure Refugia. We then spell out more specific instances which, we argue, anticipate our vision of this transnational polity.

Transnational communities

In countries that have long hosted large numbers of refugees and will likely do so for the foreseeable future – Jordan,[1] Turkey, Lebanon, Iran, Pakistan, Kenya, Ethiopia, and Uganda among others – refugees have established tenuous communities against the odds, in the face of challenging conditions, and poor prospects. These populations have links with more fortunate kin and friends in global cities further afield – not just in neighbourhoods of New York, London, Paris, Berlin, Toronto, and Sydney, but in Istanbul, Cairo, Nairobi, Johannesburg, Mumbai, Delhi, Rio, Bangkok, and many others in the 'emerging' and 'post-socialist' world, where people of diverse ethnicities and backgrounds are thrown together.

In some cases, the diasporic populations in metropolises outside the homeland are as large or larger than the population at home – for example, Toronto's Sri Lankan Tamil population is at least double that of Jaffna, the Tamils' cultural capital in Sri Lanka itself. One could say that the centre of gravity of many of the world's ethno-national groups that have become diasporized – including the Tamils, Palestinians, Kurds, Nepalis, Somalis, Afghans, and Armenians, to give just a few examples – lie outside the country of origin. So these diasporic communities already inhabit the kind of archipelagic and transnational spaces that we envisage as constitutive of Refugia.

Taken together, people in these dispersed locations create transnational communities through their diasporic connections. Indeed, transnationalism is already an enduring if not a durable solution to their displacement and dispersal: transnationalism is what displaced and dispersed people do, or have to do, to make a life worth living. The transformational step towards a transnational polity would be to move beyond an exclusive ethnic identification to a global affinity of the displaced – and of course that is a big step. Moreover, in our view, the global affinity of the displaced includes not just refugees, but also those who are or feel displaced by neo-liberal capitalism and authoritarianism and want to make a different society. Such a step involves moving beyond the deterritorialization of any one ethnic group to the constitution of new liquid identities between ethnic, religious, and national groups. In our framing, this transfiguration is from heritage identities to relational identities.

Nascent governance structures

Many diaspora groups have created transnational bodies that could serve as partial models of governance for Refugia. In some cases, transnational elections have been held that sustain viable transnational institutions.

The well-established World Jewish Congress, founded in 1936, is governed by a four-yearly plenary assembly – the last, in 2017, was attended by 600 delegates from 90 countries. Other longstanding examples of transnational refugee governance include the Palestinian National Council and the Palestinian Liberation Organization, both founded in 1964, which attempted to undertake representation of the fissiparous Palestinian population exiled from what is now Israel in 1948, and necessarily operate transnationally.

Likewise, the first World Romani Congress took place in 1971 and adopted the red, sixteen-spoked chakra (the 'wheel of spinning energy' in Hindi) as the national flag and emblem. There have been eight further world congresses drawing in representatives and delegates from many countries. The 2008 meeting was notable in passing the Roma Nation Building Action Plan, setting out a roadmap for transnational policy making and lobbying.

The Sahrawi Arab Democratic Republic (SADR) represents another instructive example. The SADR was proclaimed in 1976 in the Western Sahara by the Polisario Front, a socialist liberation movement, following Spain's messy decolonization and the subsequent partition of the territory between Morocco and Mauritania. After Mauritania rescinded its claim to part of the Western Sahara, Morocco took over that portion and constructed a series of sand barriers lined with mines (called *berms*) to mark the area under its control. The SADR holds about a quarter of the territory. It claims and calls the territories under its control the Liberated Territories or the Free Zone. A fully functioning administration and court system operate, not only in the Free Zone, but in the Tindouf refugee camps in Algeria, which house most of the Sahrawi refugee population. The SADR has its own flag, passports are issued, and the Sahrawi peseta (together with the Algerian dinar) is used widely. Views are mixed on the quality of the governance structures and practices that the Polisario has created – which Wilson (2016a) evocatively calls a 'state-movement'. Some extol what the SADR has fashioned as a pioneering and exemplary polity run by and for refugees, drawing particular attention to the prominent role of women in public affairs. Others are more sceptical of the 'ideal refugee' narrative that has emerged in some progressive circles (Fiddian-Qasmiyeh 2014).

A more recent example of transcontinental governance is the Transnational Government of Tamil Eelam, whose transnational assembly was elected in 2010 by Tamils living in more than 15 countries outside Sri Lanka in an electoral exercise that many thought was well run (Brun and Van Hear 2012). While the Transnational Government of Tamil Eelam has been criticized as a front for the defeated Liberation Tigers of Tamil Eelam, and its achievements to date have been limited, it is the *form* of this transnational representation that matters in evaluating particular prefigurations of Refugia.

We add that the technical means for holding transnational elections are becoming more and more sophisticated, as are other platforms for refugees to express their political views (Wagner 2017). Beyond diaspora-specific initiatives, efforts to strengthen migrant forums that encompass different groups of people on the move can build on already-existing transnational civil society initiatives. For instance, in responding to a call to embed migrants in the development process, the Catholic Scalabrini International Migration Network 2015, founded in 2005, with roots going back to 1887, was but one of 40 civil society networks that signed 'the Stockholm Agenda' in 2015, an initiative that was followed by 312 NGOs debating, signing, and advocating the migrants-in-development agenda.

The United Nations Relief and Works Agency for Palestine Refugees

When we think of the territories to which the Palestinians fled after the formation of the State of Israel, we immediately think of war, poverty, despair, and destruction. However, it is worth looking more searchingly at the achievements of the United Nations Relief and Works Agency for Palestine Refugees (UNRWA) and seeing it as offering an unfinished, but potentially more generalizable, model of transnational governance with refugee participation. UNRWA was set up by the UN in 1949 and began operating in 1950. In the absence of a solution to the Palestine refugee question, the UN has routinely renewed UNRWA's mandate, most recently extending it until 30 June 2020.

The Agency provides services encompassing education, health care, relief and social services, camp infrastructure and improvement, microfinance, and emergency assistance, including in times of armed conflict. It has contributed to the welfare and human development of four generations of Palestine refugees, defined as 'persons whose normal place of residence was Palestine during the period 1 June 1946 to 15 May 1948, and who lost both home and means of livelihood as a result of the 1948 conflict.' In an odd survival of patriarchy, the descendants of Palestine refugee *males*, including legally adopted children, are also eligible for registration. UNRWA services are available to all those living in its areas of operations who meet this definition, who are registered with the Agency and who need assistance. When the Agency began operations in 1950, it was responding to the needs of about 750,000 Palestine refugees. Today, more than five million Palestine refugees are eligible for UNRWA services (UNRWA n.d.).

Since UNRWA provides public goods that are normally the remit of a conventional state (including more than 700 schools with more than 500,000 students, healthcare, social services, and various forms of infrastructure), it can arguably be regarded as a quasi- or proto-state. Moreover, it is a quasi- or proto-state that operates *transnationally* across five fields of UNRWA operations – the West Bank, Gaza, Lebanon, Jordan, and Syria. The Agency is largely staffed by Palestinian refugees. These features make it of interest to us as an admittedly imperfect, but, nonetheless, real-world example of transnational governance that could prefigure that of Refugia.

'Nothing about us without us'

We conclude our discussion of governance issues by drawing attention to just three notable examples of democratic initiatives across the refugee and migrant world, which are part of a flurry of recent examples of democracy 'from below', the locus of the demand for change and self-representation being crucial to the construction of something like Refugia:

- On 21 November 2017, the Student Parliament met under UNRWA auspices for four days to discuss how best to represent the 526,000 students in schools run by the Agency in its five fields of operation. This initiative, which started in 2001, now involves direct elections in line with UNRWA's aim to decentralize and empower the refugees under its wing

• On 25–26 June 2018, a Global Summit of Refugees met in Geneva, promoted by an Australian NGO, the Network for Refugee Voices and Independent Diplomat, a New York-based NGO. The summit involved 'refugee-led organizations and refugee change-makers' and was convened ahead of the 2018 UNHCR non-government organization consultations. The meeting adopted the pan-refugee slogan 'Nothing about us without us'. As part of the preparation for the summit, regional meetings were held to feed-in refugee voices. For example, meetings in South and Central America featured refugee voices from Turkey, the Democratic Republic of the Congo, and Russia, as well as those from the Americas. Subsequent to the global summit, regional meetings were held, including the Asia Pacific Summit of Refugees

• A diverse group of self-organized refugees and migrants convened as the 'First Refugee and Migrant Parliament' under the auspices of the European Parliament on 17–18 October 2018, committing themselves to be 'protagonists in [their] own lives'. Involving representatives of over 100 refugee and migrant organizations from all over Europe, delegates shared their experiences of discrimination and integration and started to develop plans for a permanent body. The final resolution of their meeting decried the policies, practices, and pressures instigated by states and politicians against refugees and migrants – including deportations, maritime push-backs, and the externalization and militarization of European Union borders – and called for means of addressing root causes of displacement. Again, the slogan was 'No policy about us without us. We demand to be included in policy making when it concerns our lives'.

Finance

Some of these transnational forms of refugee governance are part-funded by contributions from the diaspora. More broadly, remittances by refugees to their troubled homelands and regions are of course highly significant; they have long been, in effect, a form of global redistribution of wealth somewhat akin to taxation. As is well-documented, much of this money travels through self-organized informal money transfer systems like *hawala* and *hundi* or through peer-to-peer mobile mechanisms like *Mpesa* in East Africa, which partly bypass states and formal banking set-ups (Lindley 2010). As many have pointed out, the scale of this transnational redistribution is huge, more than three times the amount of aid.[2]

The well-established means of remittance, both informal and corporate (like Western Union, MoneyGram, WorldRemit, and TransferWise), provide the backdrop against which more ambitious forms of financial connectedness can emerge. Some have started as local projects, for example, the World Food Program's blockchain-based system to distribute food and other approved items to refugees in camps. The program was piloted in January 2017 in Pakistan and works using an iris scanner (instead of cash, vouchers, or e-cards). 'Blockchain against Hunger' is already in operation in Azraq and Zaatari refugee camps in Jordan and is planned to expand to 500,000 World Food Program beneficiaries.

Given the use of e-transactions inside the camps and the common use of international remittances, it is possible to argue that many refugees are more experienced in digital commerce and finance than long-settled populations, often still locked into mono-currency cash transactions. However, the UNHCR calculated in 2017 that a key technical constraint in spreading digital technology to refugee and other deprived populations was that up to one billion people had no official identity. A body called the ID2020 Alliance pulled together corporate, government, and non-government agencies in an ambitious plan to provide a secure digital identity to everyone using blockchain and biometrics (Leong 2019).

Given strong corporate interest in this push to digitize identities (including from Microsoft), it is not surprising that several authors have expressed anxiety that the motivations for spreading the technology are suspect or, at best, mixed. The outcomes are clearly useful for donors and agencies, providing clear and accountable ways of delivering aid, controlling stock levels, and reducing corruption (or, as ID2020 termed it, 'financial leakage'). However, there is too much experimentation without consultation. Refugees are offered little in the way of data protection, initial and renewed consent, or participation in the design, modification, and outcome of these blockchain projects. Critics have suggested that 'transparency is the key' to improving humanitarian technology (Jacobsen 2017, Zak 2019). Certainly that is central, but if these experiments and experiences in using blockchain technology are to find a place in a future Refugia, full democratic control at all stages of the conception, design, and implementation of similar projects will have to be assured.

Culture and sport

Proto-Refugia also exists in the realm of culture, seen in the transnational mobility of art, music, dance, poetry, language, festivals, and sport. For example, Music Action International works with refugees and other traumatized people to transform their lives through shared musical experiences. It organizes an annual Syria Summer School in London, where over 60 young refugees from Syria, Iraq, and Afghanistan sing, dance, and play instruments. On the last occasion, a Syrian beatboxer, Palestinian dancer, Roma musicians, and others shared a 'celebration of the rhythms, traditions and melodies of the young refugees' homelands and created new work inspired by their own tastes, hopes, and aspirations for the future' (Music Action International 2018). The film *Revenir* (2018), which has won 18 awards, has become an iconic account of a refugee journey, told through the eyes, or rather lens, of Kumut Imesh, a refugee from Côte d'Ivoire living in France, who now works in the digital economy. Unusually, he reverses direction as he retraces his journey when he fled a civil war in his home country. As the promoters of the film declare, Imesh illuminates the struggle for human dignity and freedom.

In sport, a refugee team was recognized at the Rio Olympic Games in 2016 – a very modest step in the big picture perhaps, but a tacit recognition of a body of people outside nation-state affiliation. Building on this experience, and backed by UNHCR, the Olympic Refuge Foundation seeks to provide safe spaces and sports facilities in camps and refugee communities across the world (*Guardian*, 17 January 2018) (Figure 4.1).

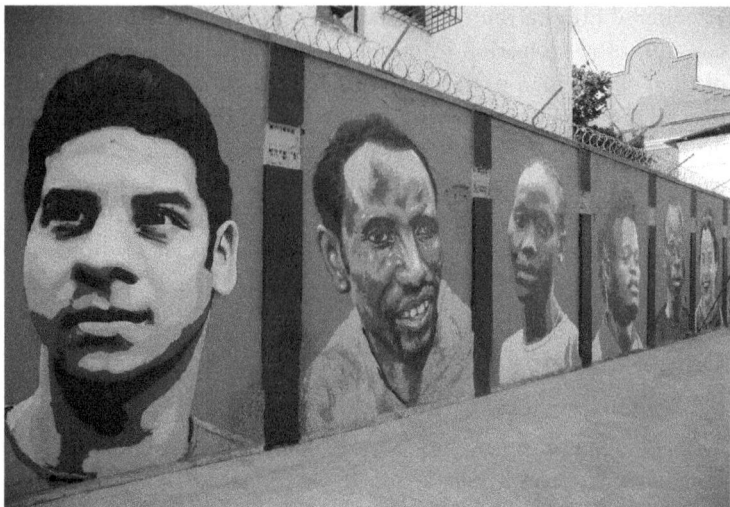

FIGURE 4.1 Mural in Rio de Janeiro depicting refugees who competed, not under national flags, but under the Olympic flag, in the 2016 Olympic games. (From Wikimedia Commons; Courtesy of Tomaz Silva/Agência Brasil.)

Other initiatives on the football pitch have also yielded fruit. An Irish volunteer and his friends help organize a Football Festival at Kará Tepé refugee camp on the island of Lesvos, Greece. According to the organizers, Football for Refugees, 'around 150 boys and girls (drawn mostly from Syria, Iraq, Afghanistan, and Eritrea) played football together each day, spread into groups according to age and gender'. The festival culminated in the creation of a new football team of refugee children, Kará Tepé United. Subsequent tournaments and festivals have provided, they say, a 'truly special demonstration of the unifying power of sport with young people from different countries, different backgrounds and different languages all united in the name of football and fun' (Football for Refugees 2017).

Creating urban communities

While sanctuary cities and cognate initiatives, large and small, discussed in Chapter 3, point to prefigurative forms of Refugia mainly in the global North, we should not lose sight of the fact that most refugees and migrants are located in the global South, often in cities and urban settlements in regions of conflict. More than 60 per cent of the displaced worldwide live in urban areas, and in some regions the proportion is much higher: in the Middle East and North Africa, where more than a quarter of the world's displaced are located, the proportion in towns and cities is between 80 and 90 per cent (World Bank 2017).

We can distinguish between two urban settings in which refugees and other migrants have created communities: cities and towns which accommodate displaced people as urban residents in particular neighbourhoods, and refugee camps and settlements which become urbanized, if not cities in their own right.

Urban neighbourhoods

The importance of ethnically based networks in urban and other neighbourhoods where refugees and other migrants gather and create communities has long been understood. Recent research has underlined the importance of such social bonds outside migrants' particular ethnic groups for the kind of economic and social cohesion that Refugia would need to foster. Researchers in three cities hosting large refugee populations – Gazientep in Turkey (Syrian and Iraqi refugees), Nairobi in Kenya (Somali and Congolese refugees), and Peshawar in Pakistan (Afghan refugees) – underscore the ambivalent role of social networks in furthering or hampering displaced people's ability to achieve self-reliance (Landau et al. 2017).

It is well known that refugees and other migrants usually engage with people similar to them – family members, co-ethnics, and co-nationals – especially in the period soon after arrival. Such networks provide accommodation, help, and advice about how to get by in the new city. Landau and his colleagues (2017: 12) argue that refugees and other migrants may be constrained from getting on as far as they might when such 'in-group' networks remain the principal locales of social life: 'Social networks – particularly those that ultimately extend beyond ethno-national "in-groups" – are central to [refugees'] successes'. Conversely, for 'some refugees, lack of access to social networks – particularly those extending to "out groups" – means remaining trapped and marginalized. This appears to be particularly the case for women, who may face stigma from their own or host communities should they reach out to strangers' (Landau et al. 2017: 12).

Comparative research concludes that over time, connections outside the migrant's or refugee's ethno-national group – especially with members of the host community – can be crucial in helping to challenge precariousness. For example, Biehl's (2014) work on the 'superdiverse' neighbourhood of Kumkapi in Istanbul – at the centre of varying migration flows for decades – points to the emergence and importance of commonalities beyond ethnicity in such living spaces. It is such trans-ethnic and cross-national bonds beyond particular ethnic affinities that Refugia will need to foster to build a coherent and dynamic new society.

Camps as cities

If there are strong traditions and practices of accommodating refugees and migrants into cities and towns, in both the global North and South, another narrative recasts refugee camps and settlements (mainly in the global South) as in themselves cities or proto-cities. In pioneering work on the Dadaab camps in northeast Kenya in 2000, Michel Agier (2002: 322) pointed to 'the novel socio-spatial form of city-camps', posing the questions:

> Can the refugee camp become a city in the sense of a space of urban sociality, an urbs, and indeed in the sense of a political space, a polis? Or why does it not manage to do so? Can it or can it not break free from its initial constraint of enclosure and oppression, as have, in other historical contexts, the townships of apartheid or the African encampments of colonial cities, which were other crippled forms of construction of the urban?

His answers seem to have been 'yes' – at least, he averred, that camps function as 'sketches or embryos of cities' (Agier 2002: 323). Similar views have been supported by those who see long-running camps as de facto cities with urban forms of social and economic life: 'camps are the cities of the future' (Kleinschmidt 2019). If many Palestinian refugee camps and settlements in Jordan, Lebanon, and elsewhere are indistinguishable from urban neighbourhoods, much the same could be said of Afghan settlements in Pakistan and other situations of protracted displacement. More recently, the Zaatari camp in northern Jordan, housing Syrian refugees in the wake of the conflict in that country, has been cast as an emergent city. While again far from perfect, another example is Camp Domiz, a Syrian refugee camp in northern Iraq that has been branded as a 'Refugee Republic'. Its inhabitants have set up community centres, shops, and places of worship. As an imaginative photo documentary by Dutch journalists shows, an urban community has emerged, attracting not just refugees, but also some of the local Iraqi population to shops and markets (Refugee Republic 2012). Like urban neighbourhoods in large metropolises, 'refugee cities' in the sense of community-led initiatives in refugee camps and settlements such as Camp Domiz can be seen as further prefigurations of Refugia (Hanappe 2017).

Some have cautioned against this view. While agreeing that camps like Zaatari indeed manifest some features of urban life, a piercing blog by Jeff Crisp (2015) warned against accepting camp life as the 'new normal'. It is worth quoting his blog at some length, since it gives a flavour of the life that refugees have created in Zaatari:

> A standard narrative has emerged … epitomized by the opening sentence of a recent Associated Press story: 'Only empty desert three years ago, the Middle East's largest camp for civil war refugees has grown from a town of tents into a bustling city.'

As Crisp notes, such journalists point to how

> The tents that were originally used to accommodate new arrivals from Syria have been progressively replaced by prefabricated caravans. Refugees have created increasingly elaborate gardens,

some of which even feature small fountains. One enterprising refugee family has established a pizza delivery service. And a vibrant marketplace has materialized in the centre of the camp, strung out along a track that has become known as the Champs Élysées.

He continues,

The impression given by such reports is not entirely inaccurate. In a very short time, Zaatari has become the fourth largest concentration of people in Jordan. Its infrastructure and amenities have steadily improved. And with the support of the Jordanian authorities and international community, the refugees have succeeded in making the camp a somewhat more comfortable place to live than when it was hurriedly established.

However, Crisp resists the 'normalization' that casting camps as cities can imply:

The notion that Zaatari is characterized by a 'new normalcy' is a very dangerous one. It is certainly true to say that the camp's residents are doing whatever they can to make the best of a very difficult situation. But it is not normal to be accommodated behind a barbed wire fence and to be deprived of freedom of movement. It is not normal to live in a situation where the entire population lacks the rights and entitlements of citizens. And it is certainly not normal to wake up each day without knowing when or even if you will ever be able to return to the place that you consider to be your home.

This cautionary note is certainly valid. As Crisp partly concedes, the cumulative development of urban communities in such settlements has a positive side, but we concur in his view that the lack of political rights and representation is still problematic. To use the language we introduced in Chapter 2, even if a modest *oikos* has evolved, a *polis* is still absent – a yawning gap that could and should be filled by linking such camps to Refugia.

Enclaves, autonomous regions, and exilic spaces

Moving from urban settings to the regional scale, a number of enclaves and proto-statelets currently host refugees, and for us in some ways prefigure Refugia. Two examples are highlighted briefly here:

The Bekaa Valley

With its long tradition of accommodating refugees (notably Palestinians), Lebanon has received at least 1.2 million Syrian refugees in the years since the Syrian conflict erupted in 2011, adding about 25 per cent to the country's estimated population of 4.6 million. Most of the refugees are self-settled in various ways, and the Bekaa Valley has turned into a temporary home for many of them. There is a substantial Lebanese diaspora scattered throughout the world, some of whom maintain homes in Lebanon as well as in the global North – in North America, Europe, Australia, and elsewhere. They may visit these homes for a few months in the year. A wealthier portion of the diaspora (particularly those in Canada) has such homes in the Bekaa Valley. There have been at least three modes of refugee 'settlement' in the Bekaa Valley that incorporate these 'second homes':

- Refugees who have a direct or indirect relation with the absentee diaspora homeowners – either as relatives or friends – live in these houses or on land attached to the houses for free or for a nominal rent
- Refugees unrelated to the owners who rent or squat on land from such absentee owners
- Refugees who rent from local and international non-governmental organizations, which have in turn rented the land from absentee owners.

These are very insecure settlements, vulnerable to demolition by the Lebanese authorities (Limoges 2017), but they nevertheless point to a promising transnational means of addressing displacement.

Rojava

The mainly Kurdish enclave in northern Syria (also known as the Democratic Federation of North Syria) is based on principles of direct democracy, non-discrimination in terms of ethnicity (it includes both Kurds and Arabs), gender equality, freedom of religion, and other familiar aspects of the Universal Declaration of Human Rights. While the proto-state reportedly has its flaws, Rojava seems to be one of the healthier developments in that troubled region. Its male and female militias helped to liberate people from Isis control. Noteworthy in the Refugia context is that the enclave has accommodated more than 15,000 refugees from the fighting in Mosul and tens of thousands of people displaced internally within Syria, despite coming under attack by Turkey and others (Knapp et al. 2016). Though often precarious, autonomous regions like Rojava show the kind of accommodation of the displaced that can be possible and point to a further prefiguration of Refugia.

Though the fit is not exact, such enclaves bear some resemblance to what O'Hearn and Grubačić (2016) call 'exilic spaces' or 'non-state spaces', defined as 'areas of social and economic life in which people and groups attempt to escape from state authority and capitalist economic processes, whether by territorial escape or by attempting to build structures that are autonomous of capitalist processes of accumulation and social control' (2016: 163). Drawing on James Scott's Zomia and 'the art of not being governed' (Scott 2009) and on other examples such as the Zapatistas in Mexico, O'Hearn and Grubačić seek structural cracks in the interstate system and the capitalist world economy in which communities practice direct democracy and mutual aid. In our vision, Refugia would be a joined-up version of such exilic spaces.

The mobile commons

Such spaces are in some ways cognate to what we referred to as the mobile commons in Chapter 2, which we characterized briefly as acts and initiatives of solidarity and mutual aid by people on the move and people through whose localities they move. We see such initiatives as precursors to the formation of the kind of affinity that Refugia would need to bind it together.

The migrant and refugee crisis of 2015–16 generated many such mobile commons initiatives. Examples include collective action by sub-Saharan Africans thrown together in emergent communities crossing the Sahara or holed up in Libya. Likewise, Syrians, Afghans, Iraqis, Eritreans, and others cooperated (along with supportive citizens) in actions on the East Mediterranean route through Turkey, Greece, and the Balkans, notably in surges to breach the borders of southeast Europe (in Turkey, Greece, Macedonia, Serbia, Hungary, Austria, and Germany). Sometimes gatherings of refugees and migrants at choke points have formed ephemeral communities and settlements, such as the Jungle, near Calais (demolished in 2016), Idomeni camp on the border between Greece and Macedonia, or Ventimiglia on the frontier of Italy and France. These actions forced temporary changes in the European migration and asylum order – however short-lived such changes have proved to be. Perhaps more sustained were the social media networks providing commentary on smuggling routes, rates, nodes, and bottlenecks as online manifestations of the mobile commons.

Self-organization of refugees at the Jungle near Calais has generated much written, literary, and visual commentary (Murphy and Robertson 2018, Agier et al. 2019, Hicks and Mallet 2019), which shows both the solidarities and tensions that emerged in this and other ephemeral refugee communities. Here, we focus on the forms of mobile commons that emerged in Greece and the surrounding region in the course of the 2015–16 mass migratory movements.

Greece: From emergent border communities to urban squats

Accounts of solidarity initiatives in Greece from 2016 give a taste of some of these 'commoning' activities. In March 2016, Europe closed off the East Mediterranean migration route in a bid to stem movement through Turkey, Greece, and the Balkans further into Europe. One outcome was to leave stranded some 60,000 migrants who had made it through Turkey into Greece and were scattered among the country's ports, cities, mountains, and islands. Tens of thousands found themselves stuck on the border between Greece and Macedonia, near a village called Idomeni, where they were subject to periodic evictions.

A report on the conditions at the Idomeni site captures the precarious and ambivalent character of the emergent border community well:

> The closing of the border undoubtedly transformed Idomeni, little by little, into a kind of small community. This was, however, a community of great contrasts. On the one hand, one could witness a massive mobilization of groups and individuals who created a solidarity network of physical and psychological support for the refugees, but on the other hand, the situation that had been created in Idomeni was full of exploitation, deprivation, physical and psychological harm and suffering (Anastasiadou et al. 2017: 48).

Frustrated at being stuck in tents, barracks, and camps, substantial numbers of refugees and migrants around Idomeni and elsewhere took matters into their own hands. Linking up with activist citizens in the burgeoning solidarity movement, they occupied a number of vacant hotels, whose owners had gone bankrupt during Greece's economic crisis. The Idomeni report recounts the move of some inhabitants away from the wretched border camp, highlighting a well-run squat in Thessaloniki, the largest city near the Greece-Macedonia border.

Despite the difficult conditions and the challenges that always tend to arise in such initiatives, the squat seems to have worked reasonably well during its short life. Beyond providing refugees with shelter and other necessities, it experimented as a space for participation and inclusion. The neighbourhood's residents seem to have accepted the squat and often provided support. An activist from Thessaloniki recalled how the squat operated:

> There was a kitchen, there were rooms, there were common spaces, there was a health centre and a storage place. ... It was an example of how immigrants can integrate in society. They all had their financial service numbers, their AMKA,[3] their card to go to the doctor. Relationships to society had been developed; a space

which had been abandoned was now being used. The squats provided good accommodation, and they annoyed nobody. ... people came [a]round, old ladies visited, they talked to the people and brought stuff (Anastasiadou et al. 2017: 73–4).

The Exarchia neighbourhood of Athens, a quarter generally experimenting with autonomous and anarchist forms of living, was another focus of squatting by refugees, migrants, and activists. Perhaps the most prominent of the dozen or so squats in and around Exarchia was the City Plaza Hotel. In some ways, the hotel was itself a metaphor for the ebb and flow of Greece's fortunes. Built in the run up to the 2004 Olympics with generous government loans obtained during boom years, the company later crashed in the course of Greece's economic crisis and the hotel fell vacant (Connelly 2016). Migrants and activists occupied the hotel in late April 2016, providing a home for some 350 refugees and migrants who had formerly been scattered around Greece. Journalists' accounts capture a sense of the atmosphere and character of the emergent community. 'City Plaza boasts a clinic, a delicious cafeteria, language classes, a café. Families live in private rooms. Some have jobs. Their kids attend Greek schools. Most of the work to maintain City Plaza is done, and decisions made, by its residents, who hail from a dozen countries and abide by a behaviour code that has zero tolerance for sexism, racism or abuse' (Crabapple 2017). Another journalist recounted that 'Daily assemblies are held in the Plaza's dining room. Amid a cacophony of Greek, English, Arabic, and Farsi, weekly rotas are decided, with the guests sharing responsibilities for cleaning, serving food and security patrols' (Connelly 2016).

An Afghan activist, himself a former refugee who had been in Greece 17 years, was one of the people that squatted in the hotel in the first place. Interestingly, he rejected the term 'volunteer', but rather referred to himself and the other activists as 'solidarians', of whom there were around 50 in the hotel, in addition to the 350 refugees and migrants from 16 countries. 'It is counter-example to the camps,' he said. 'It shows an alternative to how refugees should be housed. Not in the middle of nowhere, but in the city, with access to social services. One third of the population here are children and they are able to access schools. People should live in houses and buildings, not in camps and containers far from cities' (quoted by Patrikarakos 2018). Other activists likewise conceived the purpose to be 'to build new communities of co-existence between refugees and the local population. We don't accept that refugees should be housed in ghettos or inhumane detention centres' (Connelly 2016).

A final example of an occupation by activists and refugees in Greece we will mention is the Hotel Oniro,[4] another abandoned hotel located in the anarchist quarter of Athens. The former hotel became home to 200–250 refugees who managed it themselves with the help of activist citizens. A blog by a Palestinian refugee on the migration trail who wound up there gave a sense of how the community worked. 'The list of priorities is clear to see for everyone in the reception hall and the tasks to be carried out are equally assigned to the inhabitants, keeping the place always clean and in a tidy state'. He continued, 'A meeting gathering residents and volunteers is also held once a week to discuss basic services like [the] kitchen, pharmacy and the depot of basic supplies in addition to other services that could be provided depending on their availability' (Loubani 2016).

Conclusion

In this chapter, we have demonstrated that there are many transnational political and economic initiatives by refugees and solidarians that prefigure Refugia. These include representative bodies, remittances, and the use of 'humanitarian technology'. We have also alluded to 'state-movements' and quasi-state entities. By so doing, we are not endorsing them uncritically – for they have serious flaws and shortcomings – but simply pointing to a long and thriving tradition of transnational financial transactions, homemaking and self-governing initiatives among refugees, which show that the emergence of a transnational polity like Refugia is neither impossible nor a mere fantasy.

Turning to the transnational governance initiatives, we concede that these are limited in influence and achievement so far. But the various summits, assemblies, and the contributory meetings we have alluded to mark important moments, as they have brought together refugees from different regions and continents, and not just their representatives nominated from outside. They provide precursors to the kind of pan-refugee presentation and representation that we envisage in Refugia – beyond those forms of governance already found in particular ethno-national groups and diasporas.

We should also not over-romanticize the formation of communities in camps and squats. In particular, conditions in the Calais Jungle, Idomeni, Ventimiglia, and other border choke points were often squalid and desperate. Micro examples like City Plaza Hotel and Hotel Oniro in Athens were far from perfect. Enclaves like the Bekaa Valley and Rojava are precarious and vulnerable to state repression and eviction. But the positive side is that such mobile commons initiatives and activities feature community formation and reproduction through mutual aid sustained by refugees and migrants en route and concerned citizens working together – and they thereby constitute prefigurative forms of Refugia.

Camps and communities in countries neighbouring conflicts, neighbourhoods in global cities, transnational political practices and money transfers, emergent communities and activities in disparate locations, and initiatives by citizens and community groups: all are fragments in disparate locations that taken separately do not seem to promise much. But in the aggregate, they add up to Refugia, imperfectly prefigured. We propose that consolidating them into a common polity could prove to be a way out of the current impasse. As we suggest in the next chapter, in this vision, Refugia as a transnational, durable solution will come about incrementally and cumulatively by the collective activity of refugees and sympathetic citizens organizing in the interstices of the nation-state system and the international governance architecture. As we have suggested, Refugia will be essentially self-organized and self-managed, requiring neither political nor cultural conformity, but simple agreement on principles and deeds of solidarity and mutual aid.

VIGNETTE (2030)

'Skinny Doc' feels the sun on his face in the Elysia Refugium (Registered No. 145/2025), Somewhereland in West Asia

'Salaam "Skinny Doc", how ye going?'

Farid chuckled as the two young women went by on their way to their dance troupe, laughing while slinging their kit over their shoulders. His nickname was a combination of respect and humour. He was once a 'proper' doctor, with a brass plate on the door of a lovely old house in the Al-Jdayde quarter of Aleppo. Maronites, Chaldeans, Armenians, and Syrians all came to Dr Abadi's door. He was known for his good manners and careful diagnoses.

His house was flattened in the war, his life ruined. He no longer talked of the family he lost and the perilous journeys he took to reach Elysia, located in a Somewhereland in West Asia.

The appellation 'Skinny' is another story. His medical training was turned to good use at the request of the Assembly. He was asked to be responsible for the subcutaneous insertion of a Sesame micro-chip into anyone who wanted their rights, creds (the currency), and access codes inserted into their arm – the 'skinny' option.

Naturally, Omni and Luna, the adopted names of the two young women who had sauntered past him, had wanted skinny chips.

'Don't mess up our beautiful skins', he remembered them admonishing. They added: 'Only oldies still carry around cards and phones'.

It was wonderful seeing these confident young women emerging from the bewildered, traumatized souls who had been dumped at the refugium by some brusque Somewherelanders. Like so many other young Refugians, they had embraced what they called 'universe names' and said goodbye to the religions and ethnicities of their forbears.

The dance troupe was rehearsing their pageant called 'Surviving, Arriving, Thriving', commemorating the founding of Elysia.

Skinny Doc felt the sun on his face. His old life was buried in the ashes of Aleppo, but he had found a little serenity and ease.

Notes

1 In the last 60 years, Jordan has dealt with no fewer than six mass influxes: in 1948, 1967, 1982, and 1990 (all Palestinians), then 2003 (Iraqis) and from 2011 (Syrians, including Syrian Palestinians).
2 According to the World Bank, migrant remittances totalled US$466 billion in 2017, and the total has increased inexorably in recent years (World Bank 2018).
3 The AMKA is Greece's social security number, hence a form of ID.
4 The name is resonant for us because Oniro is related to Oneiros, the Greek word for 'dream'.

5

MAKING REFUGIA WORK

In Chapter 4, we suggested that Refugia already exists in a prefigurative, but fragmentary and highly imperfect form. In this chapter, we describe the basic principles of social justice that undergird Refugia and show how a Refugian social identity can be fostered. We then demonstrate that there are practical and credible ways of improving lives in Refugia – through homemaking, effecting solidarity, creating a smart card/app/chip, adopting innovative democratic policies, and improving livelihoods, education, healthcare, and security. As we are steadfastly committed to a conception of Refugia that grows organically from below, the suggestions we advance are just that – pointers to a future that will have to be made and remade by Refugians themselves in their everyday lives. Some suggestions are broad indicators of an orientation or direction of travel, while some are more concrete proposals. However, before discussing these practical aspects of building Refugia, we need first to sketch out some core principles underlying the shaping of a good society.

Reaching for a good society

Given its emergence from a socio-political movement for global justice, we suggest that Refugia would reach for a good society, drawing on a clear set of precepts that are the foundation of such a society – one which allows a decent life, a life worth living, for all. We are, of course, not claiming novelty here – for centuries, classical political philosophers from Aristotle to Kant have sought to grasp what a good society might be like. (For more modern accounts see Galbraith [1996] and Lippmann [2004].) Here, we try to condense the notion to its basic elements.

By a good society, we mean a society in which everyone has a decent life, a life worth living. This does not mean just security, shelter, a means of livelihood, and subsistence: in other words, survival. Nor do we mean simply a comfortable life. A 'life worth living' necessarily includes dignity, a sense of worth and purpose – for oneself, one's family, and for others with whom one has an affinity. Part of that sense of worth will likely come from a reasonable balance between private life and public life, with a sense of contributing to the common good, while allowing for the possibility of withdrawal from public life at certain stages of the life course. Since a decent life would likely involve participation in a shared endeavour, there would be an expectation (though not an obligation) to engage in public life, be it political, social, or cultural.

Again, since a life worth living can be better and more easily achieved collectively (both in the sense of the aggregate of individual actions and in the sense of conscious collective activity), there would be an obligation to contribute to collective sustenance, through taxation or the contribution of labour. This can be achieved in a number of ways including voluntary labour or as a contribution to collective insurance. The threshold of such an obligatory contribution would likely be low, but sufficient to assure a fulfilling life for all Refugians.

Engagement in public life or the public sphere involves engagement in what we have called the 'known community' (Van Hear and Cohen 2017), as well as in what Anderson (1983) called the 'imagined community'. Engagement in the known community takes place in spaces where one lives or has lived, among people one knows or knows of. It is the sphere of relations, interactions, and encounters between people, past and present – in schools, neighbourhoods, workplaces, marketplaces and shops, places of religious observance, associations and clubs, sports and leisure venues, and during cultural activity. It is the realm of associational life. The known community has some affinity with the ancient Greek notion of the agora, the open place, the gathering place, the assembly, where people meet to shop, market, buy and sell, socialize, and exchange ideas. The known community also has some affinity with the modern notion of civil society: since Refugia is multi-sited, we can speak of transnational civil society, which in turn points us to engagement in the wider imagined community, the wider collectivity brought together in the transnational polity, Refugia.

In short, a good society for Refugians would mean an assured life, rather than its antonym, a precarious life – the condition facing most displaced people today (as well as many citizens). By an assured life is meant a life that one can lead with confidence – in oneself, for one's family, one's community, and the wider collectivity, and for the future. In what follows, we provide some pointers to mechanisms that could work to achieve these aims.

The construction of a Refugian social identity

When developing the underlying concepts informing our approach (Chapter 2), we submitted that social identities are becoming more complex, more multiple, and less tied to an exclusive territorial expression. They are socially constructed, not primordial. This general observation allows us to outline the creation of a potentially unifying Refugian social identity, one that will overlay and parallel, though not necessarily supersede, prior identities. Many Refugians share the experience of a common trauma, having been displaced by violent conflicts, including civil wars and ethnic cleansing. They have, in many cases, fled for their lives. Along their journey to safety – frequently a perilous safety – they have met other displaced people with different origins. As BenEzer and Zetter (2014: 314) compellingly argue, journeys are 'powerful life-changing events'. They continue: 'Exploring the experience of the journey can shed new light on the social and individual processes of identity formation, adjustment and transition, and settlement and integration for refugees'. The authors rightly observe that for many refugees, any one journey may be followed by onward journeys and, sometimes, by return, deportation, and remigration.

Ignoring for the moment the complexity of multiple migrations, we can see, analytically, that the construction of a Refugian social identity will draw from three wellsprings:

- The trauma of displacement and the personal and social memories of those events, which remain as potent sediments in the mind and the collective consciousness
- The resilience and survival skills, as well as the need to reach out to others, developed during the journey or journeys to safety
- The processes of homemaking and community building that arise at the sites of temporary refuge or permanent settlement.

The first component, the initial trauma, suggests that, once safe, Refugians will have to deploy established techniques in creative disciplines like art, dance, drama, and music, together with cognitive behaviour therapies, not only to damp down the wounds of their harsh experiences, but also to recover the positive aspects of belonging, kinship, and family solidarity in their new settings. The second element of their emerging commonality, the beginnings of inter-group support on the journey, will be crucial in developing trust and confidence and the opportunity for permanent co-operation with other Refugians of different ethnic, linguistic, and religious backgrounds. The final and crucial element, homemaking, needs separate discussion, which we provide below.

From shelters to home

Let us start with one of the necessities of life, shelter, and to the necessary journey from canvas tents, to bricks and mortar, then to more capacious understandings of home. The standard United Nations High Commission for Refugees (UNHCR) 'family tent' has a lifespan of one year and enough room for a family of five. It is poorly adapted to extreme heat or cold. The use of this rudimentary shelter was predicated on cost, convenience, and, crucially, on the fallacious assumption that refugees would rapidly be integrated or returned to their countries of flight. There are a lot of poor (and contested) data on just how long refugees actually stay in their 'temporary' shelters. A figure of 17 years is widely cited, but is certainly exaggerated – one better estimate is that the mean duration is around 10 years (Devictor and Do 2016). Even if we accept the lower figure, it is vastly too long to spend in a standard-issue tent, so it is certain that Refugians will want, and need, more durable, dignified, secure shelters, ones that can be adapted, improved, or replaced for long-term use.

Refugians will be pleased to know that friendly designers and architects have been hard at work at producing shelters immeasurably superior to a tent. A German architect has developed an easy to assemble structure, called a Domo, while the famous Swedish furniture maker, Ikea, has come up with 'Better Shelter', a strong flat-pack house that can be assembled in four hours and includes a solar panel and a Universal Serial Bus (USB) port. While these and similar designs are improvements on tent cities, we suggest that a more long-lasting solution will be for constituent assemblies in each refugium to consider customized site-and-services schemes. To explain briefly: in such a scheme, the road network and common areas are laid out, while ducts providing drainage, sewerage, fresh water, electricity, and a fibre optic cable are supplied to designated plots.[1] The actual houses could be built by trained Refugians, with materials provided through entitlements downloaded to Sesame cards/ apps/chips (see below for a full explanation of this facility). Specialist Refugian builders and contractors will find employment in assisting novice housebuilders. The houses will be designed to allow expansion to accommodate a growing family, a new family member joining, or to reflect increased needs, like studios and other spaces for home working.

Homemaking: A gendered approach

Homemaking is both a prosaic thing – providing a sturdy shelter – and a profound thing, the social construction of a place of safety and belonging, a neighbourhood where a circle of trust, goodwill, loyalty, and reciprocity can be built. Sometimes, the rather vague word 'community' is used to express the encompassing meaning of home. For refugees to make a home in this wider sense is a daunting task. Capitalist societies – nearly all societies now – are suffused with ideas of individualization and the primacy of market relations, embodying almost the opposite values to community. Again, refugees have had little reason to trust the people around them. They have been driven from their homes, exploited by people smugglers, met by stony-faced officials, and sometimes confronted with angry locals who do not want them in their spaces.

Bearing in mind this difficult context, we recognize that the task of homemaking in exile is fraught with difficulties. It also has powerful gender dimensions. Without wishing to repeat some simplistic biological trope that women nest and men hunt, past research on exiled communities shows important gendered variations in homemaking. For example, in the case of Chilean refugees in Scotland, men were troubled by their loss of power and voice and characteristically compensated for this by an interest in homeland politics (Kay 1988). By contrast, women deeply missed the kinship and intimacy they enjoyed in Chile and sought to rebuild such relationships at the place of settlement. In a more complex reading, exile served to 'disarticulate' public and private spaces, making the gender order both precarious and necessary to renegotiate (Kay 1988: 17). For example, when men were called upon to perform domestic roles in exile, this was sometimes welcomed by their partners, but sometimes resented for undermining the honour, deference, and respect due to women. Again, those women who were used to undertaking public roles in Chile with the help of hired help at home, suddenly were confronted with having to accept the bulk of domestic and childcare responsibilities.

Refugians can also learn useful lessons from a different, more contemporary case. Women living in the refugee centres in Berlin have been usefully surveyed by Dilger and Dohrn (2016). The refugees came from Syria, Afghanistan, and Eritrea and spoke a number of languages, including Farsi, Arabic, and Tigrinya. While the researchers took full account of the ethnic, national, and linguistic variety of the women they interviewed, certain common demands emerged. Many wanted to continue their studies or find work in the occupations for which they had already trained. Others focused on immediate improvements to their living conditions and enhancing long-term opportunities for their children (Dilger and Dohrn 2016: 42). Women who had been used to relatively shielded domestic settings concentrated on re-creating such spaces. Drawing on the findings of the Berlin study, we can infer that it is important that Refugia-at-large responds both to women's demands for lockable bathrooms and toilets, for spaces for dignified breast-feeding, and to their need to go out freely into the community and to markets. In their demands for privacy, safety, and protection from violence, the domestic space becomes the public space, the personal, the political.

As discussed in Chapter 2, a gendered approach to homemaking is given a more analytical treatment in Brun and Fábos (2015: 14), who argue for a 'feminist politics of security, border management and migration'. They echo the argument that exilic politics often take on a 'masculine' form, where heroic narratives of belonging to, and making sacrifices for, an ancestral homeland drown out 'the humble creative work of domesticity in the face of politicized neglect'. It is also important to understand the rhythm of homemaking in places of refuge and settlement. As the period in camps and refugee zones becomes more protracted and the possibilities of returning to origin areas begin to fade, slowly, but surely, the heroic narratives of masculine exile politics disappear into the fuzzy past or shimmer into the distant future. Existentially, lives have to be rebuilt, children have to be fed and educated, and some kind of meaningful life and livelihood have to be refashioned. Women are likely to be at the centre of this regrounding, this replacement of displacement.

There is also a growing need to self-organize, to create some structures of representation, and engage with the world outside the camp. In a play on the word 'citizenship', Sigona (2015) calls this process 'campzenship'. He disavows Agamben's vision of the camp as a 'space of exception' where refugees are discarded or incarcerated, favouring instead a Foucauldian perspective looking at how power is constructed, socially and spatially. By using ethnographic methods, Sigona (2015: 11) shows how 'rights, entitlements, obligations and protocols are reshaped, bended, adjusted, neglected and activated by everyday practice and interactions in which the camp is not just a background but also plays a central role'.

In short, it is fallacious to assume that refugee camps, settlements, and refugee neighbourhoods and zones are only places of despair, limbo, and abjection. Certainly, that is not only what goes on there. In particular, the agentic dimensions of women's quotidian homemaking have largely been obscured by 'the male gaze'. Moreover, as the prospect of return become less and less likely, men join in and are motivated to build new structures and institutions of participation and representation. Gradually, as we suggested in Chapter 4, some features of city life can grow from a camp. However, those who believe that cities *automatically* grow from camps (for example, Kleinschmidt 2018) do not take sufficient account of the need for self-organization, democratic discussion, and representation. Refugians doing homemaking in the context of camps will need, we submit, to create a polis of some kind and reach out transnationally to secure the future viability of their new environments.

Solidarity

It is the principal task of Refugians and friends of Refugia to recognize, valorize, extend, and transnationalize homemaking initiatives, the better to generate mutual solidarity and cumulative power. This is in marked contrast to historical ways of showing solidarity with refugees, which have taken a number of forms. Where refugees have been traumatized or injured, humanitarian groups like Médecins Sans Frontières have, heroically, put themselves on the front line in delivering aid and succour. Where refugees have been stateless, far-sighted individuals like Fridtjof Nansen have persuaded states to recognize the 'Nansen Passport', ultimately issued to 450,000 people over the period 1922–1938. Where they have been friendless, the UNHCR has done remarkable work in protecting refugees across the world, winning two Nobel Prizes along the way for its efforts.

We admire and in no way seek to disparage the work of these and other refugee-friendly agencies. However, it is necessary to point out three key limiting factors to their work. First, they are required to work within the constraints of the nation-state system. This is particularly true of the UNHCR, which draws nearly all its funds from states. Second, the delineation of 'who needs what', flows from the international organization to refugees rather than from refugees to the international organization, thus severely limiting the effectiveness of voices from below. Finally, as we have already argued, current solutions predicated on the nation-state system and the current international refugee regime have reached their historical limit, a limit marked by the sheer scale of the problem, the xenophobia of politicians, and the level of resistance of long-standing residents to large-scale immigration of any description. These three limiting factors are mutually reinforcing and have propelled traditional forms of support for refugees into a lastingly reactive and demoralizingly defensive mode.

New forms of proactive solidarity with emerging refugiums can break the current impasse. These modes of engagement can be seen as four modes of 'reaching' (Cohen 2019). The first form of reaching is when we *reach down*, still locked in our positions of relative privilege, still guarding our self, and still seeing the other as other. When we *reach across,* we seek to find what we share with others, while largely sustaining our differences. 'Across', rather than 'down' because we are expressing our fellowship as much as our sympathy. It's the Fraternité of the French Revolution, or the Sisterhood of the international feminist movement. We *reach between* when we collectively create new spaces, new identities, and new social practices. We hybridize or 'creolize', the term we prefer because it escapes biological reference. Finally, we *reach inside* when we see more clearly who we are, how we have changed, and how we must change more. It is an act of inward exploration. Without being particularly conscious of our motivations, we often act without understanding that both charity and solidarity can have profound implications for our inner life. By reaching out to the other in an ever more immersive way, we can magnify the understanding and empathy that we have found in ourselves.

All four forms of 'reaching' are visible and necessary in the acts of solidarity necessary to support Refugia. The agencies, like UNHCR, and the INGOs, like Médecins Sans Frontières, will continue to reach down and extend their work, though there needs to be a radical shift in who they report to and who influences policy – away from states and funders and towards refugees. As Refugia begins to cohere, supporters can also raise funds, provide legal representation, and offer technical support.

However, the figure of the 'volunteer' prompts some rethinking in the Refugia context. The term 'solidarian' has emerged in the course of the migration upheavals of recent years to characterize politically engaged sympathizers reaching across to people on the move (Rozakou 2016: 18). This notion was taken up by activists in the City Plaza Hotel and other squats in Athens, for example, including by those who were themselves once refugees. As noted earlier, an Afghan activist with some 17 years in Greece, and prominent in running the City Plaza initiative, eschewed the idea of 'volunteer' and embraced the term 'solidarian' (Patrikarakos 2018: 69). We are attracted by this notion, which arguably implies greater and deeper political engagement than does the figure of the unpaid helper.

There is room of course for many forms of activity and solidarity. We will mention just two illustrative examples. Consider first Lesvos Solidarity (2019), which works with an open refugee camp (known as 'PIKPA camp') on Lesvos, Greece. Volunteers have provided humanitarian support, especially focusing on psychological therapy, medical help, and the delivery of food and clothing. The organization also provides language classes and play centres for children. Lesvos Solidarity has been successful in mobilizing support for refugees from backers throughout Europe and has made positive contributions to the life of the camp. Crucially, volunteers have also engaged with the local community – offering classes in vocational skills to *both* locals and refugees. This last activity is particularly noteworthy, as in many settings, locals often express resentment against the 'special treatment' accorded to refugees.

Although Lesvos Solidarity is run with sensitivity and efficiency, there is sometimes a danger that NGOs and their supporters overwhelm local government structures with the intensity of their efforts to help.[2] Local residents may also not be in sympathy with the political views that animate INGOs and their supporters. Untrammelled by the need to conform to an international mandate, Lesvos Solidarity has taken a strong political stand against the United Nations–Turkey deal to restrict migration across the Aegean and has declared a preference for world-wide open borders, a sentiment unlikely to be shared by most of the local inhabitants.

Another example of a helping community is the attempt to turn Lampedusa, the Italian island that has received many migrants and often been represented in dystopian terms, into a cultural meeting ground. Lampedusa had become a reception point and transit point from 2003, but hit the headlines in October 2013, when a boat carrying migrants from Eritrea, Somalia and elsewhere capsized offshore, resulting in 300 deaths. Local fisherfolk together with a visionary mayor responded in a humane way. Their efforts were supported by an NGO, the Askavusa Association. Using documentaries, exhibitions, and festivals, the organizers have transformed the conventional narrative, turning it from migrants as 'imperceptible bodies' – washed up, exhausted, only there to be rescued – to 'subjects of power' – with memories, aspirations, and resources (Mazzara 2016: 137). Asksavusa also engaged with the local community, successfully creating a network of activists, academics, and politicians and promoting more progressive views on migration, democracy, and the militarization of the borders to Europe (Vecchi 2016). More recently, the mood has turned sour. Echoing the turn to the xenophobic right nationally, a new mayor has turned against some of the newcomers, now described as 'Tunisian thieves', demanding restrictions to protect the island's tourist industry.

The experiences in Lesvos and Lampedusa suggest that solidarians from outside the receiving community need to face two ways – to refugees as they rebuild their lives, and to locals, ensuring that they feel empowered, not threatened, by the existence of strangers in their midst. This is a difficult balancing act and vulnerable to shifts in the external political environment. However, our notion of solidarity goes further than these experiences (though our vision was embryonically visible in both places). In our thinking, solidarians would occupy the overlapping social ecotone between Somewherelanders and refugees. In practice, as Refugia emerged, they would have the option of becoming Refugians, *reaching between* host and stranger and ultimately *reaching within* themselves, changing their own personas, attitudes, and social practices as they help to build a new, inclusive vision.

The Sesame pass/app/chip

The notion of a 'Sesame Pass' was first proposed by Robin Cohen at a panel discussion held at the Oxford Martin School in October 2015. Some significant changes have been made to the practical design, but the concept remains close to the original notion. The Sesame Pass signifies openness (as in 'open Sesame') and connection. It is a tangible object that interlaces and links all the nodes and zones of Refugia, through such elements as providing a collective identity, voting registration, legal status, labour credits, entitlements, the facilitation of work opportunities, financial transfers, and enhanced mobility.

The proposal draws some inspiration from the Nansen passport issued by the League of Nations to 450,000 stateless persons. The passport was eventually honoured by governments in 52 countries. Various certificates of identity (including a 1954 Convention travel document) were, and are, issued by national governments to stateless persons. Without wishing to disparage such certificates, which have provided support to many people in distress, many of them are no more than scrappy bits of paper. Much more sophisticated forms of digital identity, including iris scanning have been developed by the UNHCR and the World Food Program, among other agencies.

Given that refugiums will grow up in very different circumstances, sometimes in remote areas without broadband provision, it is recommended that Refugia initially adopts three alternative forms of Sesame Pass – the Sesame card, the Sesame app, and the Sesame chip, the last inserted subcutaneously (Figure 5.1).

To elaborate, the Sesame Pass will provide the following functions:

- A *secure* identification, including an iris imprint, photo, fingerprint, DNA, blood group, and a police report, where applicable. This will ensure that Refugians bearing the Pass can move without hindrance across many barriers

FIGURE 5.1 The Sesame Pass in three generations: The Sesame card, Sesame app, and Sesame chip. (Composite image created by authors. Image left: Smash icons, Image centre: 13ree.design, Image right: bsd studio. Iconfinder licences paid.)

- *Status determination*, for example, residential rights in particular refugiums or work/visitor visas for particular Somewherelands, applications for legal recognition, and progress reports on any claim for asylum in adjacent countries
- A *passport*, enabling travel to all the component parts of Refugia (the 300 or so refugiums), as well as to those surrounding and more distant states where access has been negotiated
- A *store of credits*, including materials for self-build housing, a basic income grant, Internet and phone time, and e-tickets for travel
- A *store of entitlements*, including education vouchers, access to public and e-libraries, everyday entitlements like bus passes, healthcare, food, clothing, labour credits, loans, and other banking facilities (including transfers to friends and families)
- *Work allocation and labour recruitment,* including labour credits within refugiums, advertisements for digital work, and an international labour exchange listing job opportunities elsewhere.

While the above list provides the likely uses of the Sesame Pass for Refugians, the Pass also provides a convenient way for solidarians and outside agencies of goodwill to deliver secure benefits directly to

Refugians without expensive and potentially corrupt intermediaries. Three examples must suffice:

- If, say, the Gates Foundation (which has been very active in anti-malaria campaigns) wanted to protect South Sudanese refugees living in Uganda, they could upload an e-voucher for a sprayed net to all Refugians in the area, whose Sesame Passes would be checked at a simple card reader/swipe pad at the supply points
- If, say, technical colleges wanted to provide qualifications to Refugians, they could offer access to online courses, supported by volunteer tutors, for certificates in carpentry, metalwork, plumbing, musical composition, hospitality studies, and a host of other skills
- The Sesame Pass could be developed as a digital currency in itself. While this could allow tax collection or the administration of a basic income grant for all Refugians inside Refugia, credits recorded on the Sesame Pass could also be exchanged for banknotes or other e-currencies, or used to pay taxes in Somewherelands, where applicable.

When the idea of a Sesame Pass has been discussed at various presentations, a persistent objection has been to the high level of secure identification suggested, the control it might give to the technology corporations, and the possibility of intrusive surveillance by third parties with malign objectives. The reasons for us persevering with this requirement are twofold. First, as extended functions get loaded onto the Sesame Pass, it will become a more and more valuable object, so any possibility of impersonation needs to be prevented. Second, fear of terrorists posing as refugees (even though a very rare occurrence) underlies much of the anti-refugee and anti-migrant rhetoric in Somewherelands. Without accepting the need for a secure ID, visas and travel to existing states and other sites in Refugia will be restricted by the anxieties of authorities in many states, whose goodwill is necessary to recognize or tolerate refugiums and allow mobility across their territories. However, we concur (of course) that individual rights need protection and would suggest a partial safeguard, ensuring that the local assembles (agoras) set up a judicial process run by Refugians, whereby damaged, stolen, or penetrated Passes can be reset, renewed, or replaced at the request of an aggrieved Refugian.

Democracy and governance

For smaller refugiums, the practices of direct democracy will work well for most day-to-day governance issues. Based on the old Greek agorae and the Xhosa/Zulu indabas, open local assemblies will meet on a regular basis to discuss pressing issues of the day – the provision of housing, admissions to the refugium, the mediation of minor disputes, community projects, securing water and food, and many other matters. Unlike in the agorae and indabas, there will be full gender equality, while participation by younger Refugians will be encouraged.

Where the refugium is not a small, clearly defined place, but large and perhaps fragmented, more complex systems of representation will have to be devised. From about 2010 onwards, democracies in many countries have been subverted and manipulated by foreign countries and companies harvesting digital footprints and preferences. Targeted messages, images, and false information are then deployed to support or denigrate particular candidates or parties, with no verification and no disclosure of the source of the posts. Until it was shut down, one company alone, Cambridge Analytica, had been active in 200 elections in 40 countries (Cohen 2018). This suggests that, above the level of the local assemblies, Refugians should adopt systems of sortition (random selection) to prevent electoral fraud. Such systems have many advantages – they are easy to administer, improve democratic participation, and minimize digital scams (Stone 2016, Cohen 2018). As is well known, government by lot was used in ancient Greece and has been supported under various names – 'lottocracy', 'allotment', 'demarchy' – by many writers and thinkers, including notably by Aristotle, who wrote, 'It is accepted as democratic when public offices are allocated by lot, and as oligarchic when they are filled by election' (Aristotle, Politics IV. 9, 1294b8).

To enhance democratic accountability, the terms for officeholders should be short enough to prevent the long-term accumulation of power in a small number of hands. Citizen juries should determine crime and punishment, alongside a core of qualified and experienced magistrates and judges elected with long tenure by citizen assemblies. We also suggest that transnational elections across Refugia could take place using digital voting, made simple by the use of the Sesame Pass. Elections will be to a transnational assembly and to principal office-holders. Such officeholders will represent Refugia in international forums and organizations and will negotiate with nation-states and other power containers on behalf of the polity.

Livelihoods and the economy

Refugees' resourcefulness in the economic sphere has long been recognized (Jacobsen 2005) and given added weight by recent research and debate on refugees, work, and the economy (Betts et al. 2016). Freed from the unnecessary and debilitating restriction that prohibits asylum-seekers from working, Refugians will be able to work from day one of their admission into any refugium. Where they are confronted with tent cities, Refugians could be usefully employed in erecting durable housing, laying cables, building roads and constructing schools, health centres/hospitals, market stalls, and community centres. The continuous building, replacement, upgrading, and maintenance of this infrastructure will employ roughly 20 per cent of the Fugians in the refugium.

However, as we noted in our vision of Refugia that opened this book, Refugia's economy would draw on the skills and experience of Refugians in digital commerce and services, education, and cultural and creative industries, building on expanded possibilities of various forms of distance work. The kinds of activities that are amenable to such forms of distance work include creative and multi-media projects, design, software development, writing, translation and other language services, sales and marketing support, coding, accountancy, preparation and teaching on online courses (MOOCs), and other cognate activities. Such activities are growing significantly, measured both as a proportion of the work force and in terms of value added (Graham et al. 2017). Provided that high speed and reliable broadband connections are supplied, Refugians are in a good position to take advantage of such opportunities. To reduce exploitation and the charging of high fees by existing digital platforms (like Upwork), we recommend that Refugia develops its own platform, perhaps called 'Fugiaworknet'.

Depending on context, Refugians with work visas will be able to work in many occupations in neighbouring Somewherelands.

This pattern of work already occurs in some refugee settings. What will change, as Refugia gathers negotiating power, is that the tax take can be split between a refugium and a Somewhereland, on an appropriate basis. Likewise, Refugia will be helpful in obtaining fair prices for any crops, livestock, or manufactured goods produced in a refugium that need to be marketed in Somewherelands. Where refugiums are located in sunny climes, it should be possible to partner with global energy firms to supply solar-generated energy. One model is the Noor Complex Solar Power Plant in Morocco, with a 580-megawatt capacity.

We need to add, finally, two remaining elements to the ideal of a self-sustaining economy in Refugia. First, because in some respects, the organization of work will embrace a post-capitalist ideology, *creds*, or labour credits (recorded on Sesame Passes) will be assigned for many activities that go unrecognized or undervalued in conventional capitalist economies. Child-raising, care of the sick, disabled, and elderly, tutoring, beautification, and tree planting and other green projects will all gain support (while ecologically destructive activities will not). Second, reference has already been made to remittances by refugees to their troubled homelands and regions – in effect, a form of global redistribution of wealth. As is well-established, the scale of this transnational redistribution is huge and, as refugiums become established, a good proportion of these resources from better-endowed locations will be transferred to invest in others needing support.

Shorter comments on education and security

Issues pertaining to education and security are, of course, crucial to the viability of Refugia, and we apologize for our relative brevity on these matters, largely a product of our, as yet, relatively undeveloped ideas. We can, however, provide indications of our broad lines of thinking.

Education

For practical purposes, immediate educational goals will consist of transmitting skills (like medical knowledge, construction, and translation) in workshops. Those with therapeutic experience (like shiatzu and psychotherapy) and artistic skills (like music, painting, and dancing) will be asked to take on a few apprentices. A similar arrangement will pertain to those with sporting prowess. In a more intermediate term, well-placed solidarians in distance-learning institutions (like the United Kingdom's Open University) will be asked to develop tailored modules for Refugians. The Open University already offers courses in Pakistan, Bangladesh, and over much of Sub-Saharan Africa, particularly in healthcare, teacher education, and English language teaching (Open University 2019). In time, we suggest that a prestigious Refugia International Baccalaureate, led by Refugians, should be taught digitally through distance learning and recognized across all refugiums, and increasingly in many Somewherelands.[3] The design and delivery of educational modules also have the potential to become significant ways of providing employment across the whole transnational polity as well as a means of cementing a Refugian social identity.

Security

Sadly, Refugians will have to prepare for outbreaks of violence, including xenophobic violence directly by some reactionary Somewherelanders towards the very existence of a nearby refugium and, within the polity, outbreaks of domestic violence, criminal violence, and intergroup conflict. With respect to external hostility, we anticipate that Refugia will lead to an abatement of hostility by previously angry Somewherelanders, as they sense that any perceived threat to their way of life is no longer visible and immediate. The development of social ecotones where more open-minded Fugians and Somewherelanders can meet, work together, and enjoy cultural exchanges will also dampen and cushion conflict. Nonetheless, we suggest that the UN might provide peace-keeping forces to protect refugiums in the intermediate future, pending the training of local defence forces. As for internal violence, we suggest that a small corps of professional police officers (ultimately under the control of local assemblies) be trained by trusted outside officers, using existing development assistance programmes. Community service officers (like jurors and officials) will be selected by lot and help to defuse minor forms of criminal conduct and less serious forms of violence.

Conclusion

In this chapter, we have addressed the question 'how can this work'? We argue that the core principles of social justice must underlie the construction of any new society. We are completely open in saying these are matters of morality and ethical choice. But such foundations also have practical consequences. We already know that more equal societies tend to have better outcomes in physical health, mental health, drug abuse, education, imprisonment, obesity, social mobility, trust and community life, violence, teenage pregnancies, and children's well-being (Pickett and Wilkinson 2009). It is a reasonable surmise that a more just society will lead to a more engaged civic life with fewer resentments and lower levels of conflict. We have shown how a relational identity can be constructed alongside heritage identities and how homemaking is a complex, gendered process and not just a matter of providing good-quality shelters.

We have also offered many practical suggestions regarding forms of solidarity, developing a smart card/app/chip, as well as what might work in fostering democracy and improving livelihoods, education, healthcare, and security. There remains only the need to re-emphasize that these remarks are not a blueprint, but a menu of submissions by two committed solidarians. Ultimately, it will be for Refugians to make their own societies in their own ways.

VIGNETTE (2027)

Workshop on creds and distributed ledger technology involving 20 refugiums

The delegates swept into the circular room, holding their Sesame chips near to the contactless reader and seeing their IDs flash up on the interactive whiteboards surrounding the group.

As Refugia had mushroomed – there were now over 250 refugiums worldwide – the various uses of distributed ledger technology had proliferated. The workshop was being held first, to learn best practice from the different refugiums and second, to try to encourage some convergence in protocols and Community Benefit Ratings. Everyone here was digitally smart, but some were off the scale.

Jennie the Génie (as she was known) got straight into it. 'Let's summarize what we've got now'. Four points appeared on the whiteboard:

1. To date, Refugia has issued 22.4 million digital identities through its Sesame card/app/chip.
2. Nearly all refugiums (94 per cent) have adopted the universal Refugian currency 'creds'.
3. The word has been shown to work well in a number of languages and suggests credit, belief (trustworthiness), and credentials (that is, our IDs and access codes).
4. We all pretty much agree (97 per cent of refugiums) that everyone should be allocated 10,000 non-transferable creds when they are accepted as members.

She turned on her heels and demanded: 'Afamefuna, what has your working group got for us on CBRs?'

A thin bespectacled young man started talking and scribbling on his digital pad as his words and calculations appeared on the whiteboards. 'We have counted 6,735 occupations in all the existing refugiums. To assess their Community Benefit Ratings, we have used 40 criteria, each on a continuum, as follows: Hard/Easy, Skilled/Unskilled/, Smelly/Fragrant, Necessary/Unnecessary, Prosaic/Creative, Green/Eco-unfriendly ...' he rattled on, never losing his pace and intensity for a second. 'Each point on the scale has been objectively calculated, then modified using random survey data. From this, we have developed this dynamic heuristic algorithm'.

All 40 delegates looked intently at the board, which used an updated version of Kuratowski's theorem, branching into a decision. They excitedly shouted their corrections and suggestions for nearly two hours. Finally, Jennie the Génie intervened: 'So, in sum, using the agreed algorithm, we can assign x amount of labour service creds automatically, while eliminating the possibility of corruption and self-importance inflation'.

'Yes', said Afamefuna 'and the demand/supply adjustments and collectively decided re-evaluations can easily be programmed in. And, hey, I forgot to say the Gini coefficient never gets higher than 0.1'.

'Time for a break, Fugians'.

Notes

1　Site-and-services schemes have been tried in many countries, usually as a means of improving slums. One common problem is that new homes are traded, resulting in speculation. To offset this flaw, we suggest that constituent assemblies in each refugium vest ownership in a local collectively managed trust and accord 10–50-year leases on site-and-services houses, the period varying with context and circumstances.

2　This phenomenon was observed in extreme form in Aceh, Indonesia, after the horrific tsunami in December 2004, when 164,000 people lost their lives and around 500 NGOs bearing very large sums of donated money engaged in relief and recovery efforts alongside local Acehnese government agencies and community organizations. It was difficult to track money spent, NGOs took on complex tasks they could not achieve and co-ordination with governmental officials was fitful or non-existent (Pandya 2006). Additionally, micro-territorial disputes and providing food and lodgings for the NGOs distorted local economies and threatened local social conventions. Nothing so deleterious has arisen in Greece or Italy – where many displaced peoples have been received – but the experience in Aceh (and also in Haiti, Sri Lanka, and other places) stand as stark warnings to NGOs to work in a modest and respectful manner.

3 Maha Shuayb at the Centre for Lebanese Studies in Beirut is already developing such an idea (Shuayb and Brun forthcoming).

6

SUMMARY AND ENGAGEMENT WITH CRITICS

The vision, in summary

It is Monday, 1 July 2030. The floor of the General Assembly has witnessed many unusual events. In 1960, Union of Soviet Socialist Republics President Khrushchev took a shoe off and banged the table to emphasize his displeasure with a delegate's views. In 2009, Libya's President Muammar al-Qaddafi ignored his 15-minute deadline and sermonized for 96 minutes. However, even seasoned diplomats and observers have never seen or heard anything like the joyous celebrations and tumultuous hand-clapping following the adoption of the Constitution of Refugia. The Constitution has just been unanimously approved by 1,898 delegates to the Constitutional Assembly of Refugians from all over the world. The UN Declaration of Human Rights, the Charter of Fundamental Rights of the European Union, together with key provisions of the South African Constitution have informed the work of the Constituent Assembly of Refugians, but there are many aspects of Refugia that are unique.

Stuck in their old ways, journalists are struggling to describe what has just happened. They are having to get their heads around the idea that Refugia is not a new nation-state or single legally defined country, but rather a transnational or cross-national entity, a set of connections between different sites developed through initiatives mainly taken by refugees and displaced people themselves, with some support from sympathizers. Confederal and archipelagic in character, it has joined together refugee communities in territories and neighbouring societies in conflict, those in enclaves in transit countries, and other refugees in more distant countries of settlement.

Using utopian thinking, Refugia is, in part, the outcome of an implicit grand bargain – among richer states and emerging countries, countries neighbouring conflicts, and, crucially, refugees themselves. After local discussions in local assemblies and meetings with representatives of Refugia, new constituent zones (they are called refugiums) are, in effect, licensed by the nation-states within whose territories they lie. Though subject to the host states' laws, they are autonomous zones created from below. They are self-governing and several are already self-supporting.

The result is that refugees are no longer primarily the responsibility of the nation-state that 'hosts' them, but belong to the newly formed entity – Refugia. Refugians maintain several affinities: as well as their affiliation to Refugia, they can be long-term residents of the states that license their territories (refugiums) and might also maintain nationality claims in their countries of heritage. Refugians who hold what is called a 'Sesame' identity card or chip, or can access a Sesame app, can move among different parts of Refugia, and, where negotiated, travel to long-established sovereign nations.

Refugia is governed by a transnational virtual assembly, elected by Refugians from all the constituent components of the polity. This digital structure represents Refugia globally, but there are also periodic face-to-face global parliaments. The democratic heart of Refugia comprises constituent assemblies in each refugium, feeding into its global governance, while representing the interests of local Refugians to the host society and channelling any concerns of the host society back to Refugians.

Refugians already pay taxes or contributions to the nation-states within which they live, but also to the wider Refugia polity. A portion of the latter revenue provides support for those who choose to stay in their regions of origin and has sometimes been used to leave such regions – in a similar manner to the way in which remittances have long been deployed. Revenues are also redistributed from richer to poorer parts of Refugia, though it will take quite some time to iron out the evident disparities.

There are promising signs of a new pan-Refugia identity emerging. Although individual refugiums are still marked by dominant heritage identities, the Constitution of Refugia is not based on ethnicity, language, nationality, or religion. The experience of conflict and displacement has convinced many Refugans of the fallacy and dangers of basing communities solely on such identifications. Moreover, people have been of necessity pressed into collective activity across such affiliations by their experience of forced mobility and its aftermath. Differences are respected, but Refugans claim they will create a new kind of belonging that is democratic, inclusive, and based on evolving social identities – not on prior affiliations and ascribed characteristics.

While many Refugans are wary of embracing too many of the trappings of statehood, Refugia has adopted existing symbols of belonging, like a refugee flag and anthem (designed and composed in 2018). The Constitutional Assembly has agreed to ambitious plans to extend its participation in international global sporting competitions, cultural events, international bodies, and political forums. A Constitutional Court for Refugia has been established to mediate disputes. The Constitutional Assembly has also asked the UN to allow it to switch from its current observer status to recognition as a full member. Although the request has come from a polity that is not a nation-state, nearly all the members of the Security Council have agreed and many UN-watchers are hopeful that Refugia's request will succeed.

Addressing our critics

Our vision for Refugia, which is summarized above, has evolved over five years. We have presented the idea jointly and individually at more than 20 forums of different kinds to researchers, policymakers and practitioners, refugees, and interested members of the public in Europe and Africa and have also given the idea an airing in North America and Australia. We have spoken at conferences, in seminar rooms, and on public platforms. On every occasion, we have invited criticisms and questions and refined and modified our proposal as we have proceeded. Because of the continual iteration and development of our proposal, some reactions and critiques have become heavily intertwined with earlier versions and replies.[1] What appears below is a consolidation of our responses.

Broadly speaking, our proposal has elicited two kinds of reaction. The first is to find the idea curious, intriguing, and, even if not wholly convincing, a useful way of thinking about a putative future for refugees and more generally about what a transnational good society might look like. Commentators with this sort of reaction have often asked for more detail on how it will all work. The second response is scepticism and suspicion, shading into outright condemnation – in this perspective, Refugia is at best a cop out and at worst a betrayal of refugees, an abhorrent mechanism of containment and domination (Buxton et al. 2017, Barbelet and Bennett 2018, Crawley 2018, Lutz 2018). Here, we reflect further on the concerns of critics, providing our fullest attention to the more negative critiques.

Refugia lets nation-states off the hook

A common critique is that, were Refugia to be established, it would absolve nation-states both individually and collectively from fulfilling their responsibilities to displaced people. Nation-states frequently create the very conditions that lead to displacement and should clear up their mess, this argument rightly goes. Moreover, nation-states have signed up to international legal instruments that oblige them to protect refugees. This may all be the case, but calling on nation-states to step up seems misplaced at best and naïve at worst. Nation-states have rarely fulfilled their responsibilities to refugees set out in international law: the settlement of Vietnamese boat people over the period 1975–1995 is a partial and rare exception.[2] The nation-state system certainly creates displacement, but neither nation-states individually nor the international order collectively are more than fleetingly disposed to resolve the conflict and displacement that they create. And with the world the way it is now, there is almost zero prospect of states fulfilling their obligations. How many more decades must Palestinians,

Sahrawis, Afghans, Somalis, Sudanese, Rohingyas, Eritreans, Tamils, Kurds, Congolese, and many other displaced people have to wait for nation-states to resolve their plight?

An alternative direction is some kind of self-initiated, self-empowering, and self-managed approach – and this is what we are proposing with Refugia. We argue that it is better for displacees and their supporters to step away from the current setup, accumulating the power and capacity to manage their own affairs in a new kind of polity that seeks accommodation with the nation-state system at arm's length – however uneasy such an accommodation may be. Refugia would thus seek to assure a just society and a decent life in the interstices of the nation-state system.

Who and where?

Commentators were sometimes confused as to who would constitute the population of Refugia. This, at least somewhat, was our failing, as in presentations we sometimes elided the difference between refugees and other migrants. In part, this was a deliberate conflation. As is well known, it is often difficult to distinguish between refugees and other migrants, not least because the conditions driving movement can be similar, and because people with different motivations to move often travel together and wind up in the same communities. In Chapter 4 of this book, discussing prefigurations of Refugia, we show how the mixed flows of migrants and refugees in practice result in mixed communities.

The conflation between migrants and refugees also derives from our vision of Refugia as an inclusive polity that could accommodate different kinds of people who both need a home and are motivated to build a new society. Hence, we also would want to include within the Refugian fold sympathetic citizens and volunteer helpers – we prefer to use the term solidarian – who want to contribute to the emergence of a visionary society.

The 'who?' question is related to the 'where?' question. This is, of course, a key challenge, since, as Keating (2018: 28) points out, 'Every spot on the earth's landmass, outside of Antarctica, is claimed by a country – and sometimes … by more than one. The map is all filled in'.

Rather than creating a completely new sovereign space, as foreseen in some of the single territory proposals outlined in Chapter 3, we are suggesting that Somewhereland states could be persuaded to cede some of their territory as refugiums are formed, and even to allow Refugians to live alongside Somewherelanders in neighbourhoods in Somewhereland. The first possibility raises the issue of what happens to the Somewherelanders who may be on this land already. The historical record is admittedly not encouraging – the dire fate of the Palestinians and aboriginal peoples in North America, Australasia, and elsewhere spring to mind. Somewherelander inhabitants of a given refugium would need to be persuaded that the prospect of a peaceable contiguous society is sufficiently attractive to allow Refugians to stay – perhaps difficult, but not impossible.

The second possibility – that of Refugians living alongside Somewherelanders in Somewhereland neighbourhoods – raises the issue of different statuses for Refugians and Somewherelanders: for example, long-term residence in Somewhereland for Refugians short of Somewhereland citizenship. Refugians might be persuaded to accept such denizen status in return for the possibility of living in Somewhereland. Again, some kind of dual or parallel status for such neighbourhoods in which both Somewherelanders and Refugians live could be envisaged. These neighbourhoods within Somewhereland would be part of the overall Refugia polity. These intermediate statuses are, however, compatible with our adoption of the concept of social ecotones, which allows and recognizes overlaps, enclaves, and partial separations.

Rights, citizenship, law, and power

Many other questions about citizenship, membership and rights often came up in the course of discussion. Would Refugians be citizens, and if so, citizens of what – Refugia as a whole, the particular refugium in which they are based, or the Somewhereland state in which the refugium was located? If not citizenship, what would be their status in the Somewhereland state in which their refugium was located? Would being a Refugian be inherited by descendants? Could one move from being a Refugian to a Somewherelander?

In related observations, critics also raised the issue of who or what would uphold Refugians' rights, not least in the context of potentially hostile Somewhereland neighbours. How would such rights be assured across different parts of the Refugia transnational archipelago? Would similar rights for Refugians apply across the whole of Refugia? Some saw the danger of a hierarchy of statuses, in which being a Refugian would be at or near the bottom. It was pointed out that the durable solutions envisaged the end of refugee status, while Refugia appeared to perpetuate that status – or at least the refugee identity.

Related points were raised about the application of law across Refugia and Somewhereland states. Would the same laws apply across the whole of Refugia? To what extent would the laws of Somewhereland states apply in the particular refugium that they hosted? What if people in a particular refugium started practices that were against the laws of the Somewhereland state in which they were located? Child marriage, forced marriage, and the abuse of women were referred to in this connection, as were other illiberal or authoritarian tendencies.

These are all good questions, to which we do not have complete answers. Some of these challenges may be addressed by existing principles and practices – in particular, the principle of subsidiarity and the arrangements for autonomous regions. Subsidiarity implies the greatest possible devolution of powers to a given administrative unit. Many current autonomous regions in sovereign states have such devolved powers. Refugia would build on such experience, so that one could imagine that some Somewhereland laws would pertain at certain levels – covering national security and the provision of basic services, for example – while other legal provisions became the responsibility of Refugia administrations.

More generally, rights and entitlements in Refugia would need to be consistent with the constitution of Refugia and the principles for a good society that we set out above – summed up as a life worth living for all. While we recognize many difficulties and challenges in realising a good society, in our view, this would minimize illiberal practices of the kind that objectors raise to our vision of a transnational polity.

We assume that all the constitutional provisions of Refugia will apply to those who have chosen to belong, together with the children under their care. The status is not conferred by descent, but by self-election, followed by recognition in assemblies of Refugians. We assume that, as an age of majority is reached (16 or 18, or whatever is determined by Refugians), a young person in a refugium can chose to affiliate or leave. As we note below, we further assume that there will be free movement between the refugiums for temporary purposes, but assemblies in individual refugiums will determine the rules of permanent residence. We have repeated the word 'assume', as Refugians will make such decisions and parley with their neighbours, not us.

By emerging alongside the existing nation-state order, perhaps Refugia opens up a way to finesse the rights debate. After all, the record of nation-states and international organizations in upholding rights is patchy, to say the least, and especially in the current climate: arguably, reliance on such authorities to uphold rights is misplaced. Rather than thinking in terms of rights upheld (or not) by states, we prefer to underscore the accumulation of capacity to self-manage a just society assuring a decent life in a transnational polity positioned in parallel to the nation-state system. Moreover, there is no intention to create an either/or choice; rather the rights conferred by belonging to Refugia will be additive and complementary, not exclusive. We remind our questioners that, in our vision, becoming a Refugian would be a voluntary act.

Mobility or containment: 'Another Nauru'?

Further related questions arose around movement to Refugia, within Refugia, and between Refugia and Somewhereland states. How would those who need refuge get access to Refugia, and could everyone who needed refuge be accommodated in Refugia? How would movement among different parts of Refugia work, particularly if there are disparities among them in terms of security and in living conditions and prospects more generally? Would movement be possible between Refugia and Somewhereland states that host refugiums?

We take an excursion into literature to provide us with inspiration to address these challenges. In some ways, Refugia resonates with the picture created by Mohsin Hamid in his novel *Exit West* (2017), which, given its echoes of our own thinking, we read with great interest after the initial development of our ideas of a transnational polity.

With social scientists and novelists thinking along the same lines at more or less the same time (in the wake of the 'refugee crisis'), perhaps this is an idea whose time has come – an outcome of what could be called social science fiction (Frase 2016). In the novel, people fleeing conflict in a world of upheaval move to safer locations through portals which seem to appear arbitrarily and offer conduits to different locations. Agents seem to know the locations of these portals. Though we might wish for such portals as a means of gaining access to Refugia, less magical means of access to the transnational polity are needed. One might be to enlist the services of agents who are prepared to act as facilitators of movement in benevolent rather than exploitative ways and to persuade nation-states that managed movement to refugiums in this way is preferable to chaotic movement.

To address these questions more directly, in our vision, being a Refugian implies membership of the whole Refugia transnational polity, which, in turn, implies access to any of the territories than make up that polity. We recognize that the Somewhereland states in which particular refugiums lie might prohibit, or only selectively allow, some movement. But we suggest that Somewhereland states could be persuaded to accept such pan-Refugia membership and access in return for resolution of the many aspects of displacement they would otherwise have to deal with, specifically by ceding territory in which Refugians will live.

As for Refugian citizenship of the Somewhereland state in which their refugium lies, this would be a matter of negotiation – not an entitlement. As already suggested, some forms of long-term residence in Somewhereland short of citizenship would be a more likely outcome than full citizenship. This is of course the position of many denizens currently. Many people have a set of overlapping memberships and entitlements.

A common concern is that Refugia could easily lead to the international ghettoization of refugees, confined to reservations on poor quality land that no-one else wants, without means of generating income to create decent communities, and lead a life worth living: 'another Nauru'. We recognize the danger of such dystopian nightmares – one such indeed unfolded in 2017–18 on the borders between Myanmar and Bangladesh. The key difference in our vision is that Refugia would be more than the sum of its isolated parts, with the option of mobility among its constituent territories as their political and economic circumstances ebb and flow. Refugians would also be more active, and ultimately dominant, in the shaping of their new environments.

The allusion to 'another Nauru' by our critics refers to the detention centre for asylum seekers established on this Pacific island (and a similar one established on Manus Island) by the Australian government. The conditions in the centres are lamentable, the private companies tasked with administering them swindled Australian taxpayers and have a poor record in providing medical care, safety, and freedom from sexual abuse. It goes without saying that we regard such off-shore detention and processing centres as odious. Whatever redeeming features we can point to, concern the galvanization of NGOs in Australia around issues of social justice and the mobilization of the detainees on Nauru and Manus as significant political actors in their own right. This story has been documented by a remarkable journalist and an Iranian-Kurdish refugee currently himself held on Manus Island, Behrouz Boochani (2019). His reports, together with the demonstrations of the detainees, have led to the improvement of conditions, the resettlement of all the children in detention, and an inquiry in the Australian Senate. What we take from this experience is that, even in the most adverse of circumstances, remediation comes from the self-organization of refugees and solidarity with them. Refugia magnifies this idea and takes it many steps forward.

More generally, we envisage liberal movement among refugiums (the component parts of Refugia), with some mechanisms developed for equitable distribution of people over time given disparities between Refugia locations in terms of wealth and resources. In other words, Refugians would have the option of moving to other parts of Refugia if they were not happy in a given refugium. Moreover, in our vision, being a Refugian would not be compulsory: they need not join and can freely exit. Those who do not see their future in Refugia could continue to take their chances with the asylum system of the existing nation-state order (and its limited upholding of their rights).

As for movement between Refugia and host states, this would have to be negotiated both at the level of the transnational polity and between individual refugiums and the states that 'host' them. We acknowledge that this option may be far from perfect, but it would at least provide an improvement on the current practices of containment and incarceration. The likely outcome will be the issue of visas for different purposes (tourism, work, access to health facilities, and so on) and over different periods. We do not minimize the difficulties involved, but equally, we do not think that the obstacles to such movement are insurmountable.

Refugia assumes a commonality among refugees that does not exist and is not desirable

A number of critics are rightly sceptical that displacement alone would be sufficient to bind together the populace that would make up the Refugia transnational polity. Why would a Rohingya refugee in Bangladesh identify with a Syrian refugee in Turkey? Most refugees ultimately want to escape refugee status by regaining full citizenship either through return to their homeland or by making a new home in a new nation-state. Moreover, Refugia appears to assume a kind of unity that is lacking, given divisions of class, ethnicity, gender, generation, and other social cleavages among the displaced, not to mention deep-seated enmities generated in the course of prior conflicts. And how would inequities across the different locations that comprise Refugia be addressed?

As we have acknowledged in earlier chapters, Refugia would indeed have to contend with such challenges so as to create a good society in which diverse Refugians are assured of a decent life, as well as forging a common identity and purpose. We think that this shared identity and resolve will begin to coalesce in the course of the formation of Refugia. We see Refugia emerging organically and cumulatively from a socio-political movement which brings together the disparate solidarities and transnational practices that we can see in evidence today. Those practices and solidarities already embody commitments to various kinds of social justice, imperfect and incomplete though that may be. Refugia will only emerge if there is a political, intellectual, and, not least, emotional investment on the part of displaced people and supportive citizens who relish the idea of creating a new society that draws strength from its transnational character.

As well as ethnic and religious divisions, there would of course be differences between men and women, young and old, the educated and less-educated. All societies have to deal with such challenges, and Refugia would be no different. The education system would be crucial here. We support the idea of common qualifications like a baccalaureate that would be recognized across Refugia and incrementally in Somewhereland states too (Shuayb and Brun forthcoming). But primary schooling would also be crucial in inculcating an inclusive Refugian identity, which would tolerate differences, but also provide common ground. Language would also be key. At the risk of ethnocentrism, a form of English might be the most feasible official language, but we might also imagine the emergence of some kind of Refugian Creole that draws on English, French, Spanish, Arabic, and maybe other languages common to areas from which Refugians are drawn.

We are also mindful that unlike the current refugee order, which tends to segment and separate refugees according to their different backgrounds, the founding principles of Refugia will valorize and support intercultural communication and co-operation. Enhanced sensitivity and multi-culturalism have been found to reduce ethnocentrism (Dong et al. 2008). Additionally, we anticipate that the performing arts (dance, drama, and music) and other creative expressions (including orature, literature, poetry, art, creative play, design, and puppetry) will permeate each refugium, improving the depth and pervasiveness of intercultural interactions.

The viability of such a transnational polity is doubtful

As well as the need for a shared vision and shared values to bring out a common identity and sense of purpose among Refugia's populace, the transnational polity would of course need to be economically viable. Could such a society exist alongside a world of nation-states and global capitalism that seek to subsume all? Our utopianism is pragmatic enough to recognize that there would have to be compromises, not least on the economic front, and especially in the early stages. Hence, some Refugians may indeed have to accept exploitative conditions in host states (as is the case now). Over time, though, the construction of the physical and digital infrastructure of each refugium, remittances from kin and family-members, distance work involving digital services and products, and the employment associated with the internally generated economy and administration would diminish such dependence, leading to the emergence of a self-sustaining green society and economy. Rather than submitting solely to the vagaries of the market and the commodity, the economy would be geared to *provisioning*: supplying things that people need and value, giving greater pleasure and meaning to work. As O'Hearn and Grubačić (2016: 153) put it, value would reflect 'what people choose to exert time and effort into producing, whether material or not'. Guided disbursal of surplus into communities would be aimed at strengthening Refugia's autonomy in the face of the predations of nation-states and world capitalism. The multi-sited nature of Refugia will be an asset in the creation of a transnational good society over time, not least in making possible a measure of redistribution of resources across its constituent sites.

Refugia does not address global structural imbalances and the violence they embody

Perhaps the most fundamental criticism is that Refugia does not address the root causes of displacement and indeed other forms of mobility. In this critique, Refugia appears to be a palliative initiative, neglecting structural conditions, the geopolitics of power, the violence of borders, the racial character of displacement, and other systemic dimensions: in short, it is not a 'radical solution' at all. We accept that the emergence of Refugia would not directly address the causes of displacement, which indeed derive from the skewed distribution of power globally. But we do see Refugia as potentially challenging the global order. It would do this by developing an alternative polity alongside the nation-state system, in the apertures of that system. This would be accomplished cumulatively and incrementally without sudden rupture, a gradualist strategy that could see the emergence of a regime somewhere between open borders and free movement within regional associations of nation-states. We see Refugia as a form of alter-globalization (Evans 2008) and as a global consolidation of exilic spaces (O'Hearn and Grubačić 2016).

Some critics asked, if you are thinking along utopian lines, why not go the whole way and advocate open borders? Given the persistence of nation-states for the foreseeable future and the current resurgence of nationalism and populism, we see the prospect of a negotiated mobility within Refugia and among refugiums and their surrounding states as both preferable and far more likely, while being considerably less dangerous than open borders. With totally free movement, it takes little imagination to think of displaced people being assaulted in populist outbursts of xenophobia and murderous violence. At root, the demand for open borders rests on similar illusions about the generosity of the population at large that we have discounted on the part of the leaders of nation-states. Perhaps people in general are more open-hearted than the politicians who speak in their name, but, given we are talking of peoples' lives, relying on that supposition is too much of a gamble.

Descriptive or prescriptive?

Finally, several commentators wondered if our vision of Refugia was descriptive – that is to say, describing a polity that could *actually* emerge – or prescriptive – that is to say, advocating a kind of polity that we would *like* to see emerge and would support. Again, we have somewhat conflated the two perspectives in our presentation of Refugia. We are indeed advocating the emergence of a particular kind of society, with features that we would wish to see, including forms of horizontal democracy, tolerance, equity, and transparency: the kind of good society that we outlined in Chapter 5. At the same time, this vision of an ideal society is tempered with a degree of realism, in that we see Refugia as a society that feasibly could emerge, given foreseeable conditions, including the persistence – whether we like it or not – of the nation-state system, the number of displaced people, and the paltry results delivered by the current international refugee regime. This is what we mean by pragmatic utopianism.

Concluding remarks

We have not fully addressed every one of the apposite objections to, and perceptive critiques of, Refugia. Indeed, we do not have answers to many of them. We hope though that we have given some indication of ways some challenges might be handled. Our broader aim has been to use utopianism as a method to rethink the solution to displacement in terms of the creation of a new kind of transnational polity, and in doing so, to imagine what a life worth living and a good society might look like in such a new entity.

In our vision, refugees, other migrants, solidarians, and Somewhereland dissidents will incrementally develop in Refugia a transnational good society in which people and communities can thrive. Utopian thinking offers an opportunity at least to dream of such a society and its challenges. Somewhat to the surprise of some critics, we do not shy from the jibe that we are utopian. Indeed, we happily accept that label, though with a qualification. Refugia embodies a 'pragmatic utopianism' which squares the apparently contradictory and at times antagonistic interests of Somewhereland states and Refugians.

We must ask one more question of ourselves. What if we are like the apostle Paul, only seeing through a glass darkly? What if our vision is blurred and the outcome of our ideas incomplete? Suppose, for example, that only 20 structures like our refugiums connect with one another, not hundreds, as we have imagined. Suppose the task of creating a new transnational political entity falters and, instead, the self-organization of refugees and efforts to support them result in a vigorous global social movement, but not a polity.[3] Would we then be disheartened or bereft? Of course not. Refugia is about lifting our heads above the real to fashion the imagined. It is about rejecting the attitude that says 'nothing can be done' in favour of finding alternatives that rise to the scale of the challenge. Refugia is not a promised land, indeed not a land at all, but a promising new path through the thicket of inertia and convention.

Notes

1 For this reason, it would be misleading as well as being pedantic to list comments and responses one-by-one in date sequence. To complicate matters, we have also taken on board comments by the anonymous referees reviewing our book proposal. Access to the public critiques is provided using the search term 'the Refugia project'.

2 It is perhaps worth remembering the special features of the Vietnamese case. Most of the 800,000 boat people were ethnic Chinese, for whom a special

responsibility was felt in Hong Kong, Taiwan, and Singapore. The USA and France had waged unsuccessful colonial and anti-communist wars in Vietnam, and they acknowledged some responsibility for the welfare of their former allies there. The Cold War was raging at the beginning of the period, so the USA could use its generosity to the Vietnamese refugees for political purposes. For its part, the UK-administered Hong Kong and was under moral pressure to relieve the situation in its colony. Finally, seeing desperate boat people on our television screens was then very unusual, and many citizens in Asian, European, and North American countries responded sympathetically to their plight. Sadly, compassion fatigue has now burgeoned in many quarters and is something all humanitarians have to recognize, even if we feel mortified that it even exists.

3   This outcome was suggested, indeed preferred, by the eminent Australian political theorist, John Keane, in his discussion of our idea in Sydney, February 2019.

REFERENCES

Agier, Michel (2002) 'Between war and city: Towards an urban anthropology of refugee camps', *Ethnography*, 3 (3), 317–41.

Agier, Michel et al. (2019) *The Jungle: Calais' camps and migrants*, Cambridge: Polity Press.

Aleinikoff, T. Alexander (2017a) 'Repairing a broken international refugee regime'. *Presentation at a Conference on the Global Refugee Crisis Organized by the UCLA Center for the Study of International Migration*, Los Angeles, https://www.youtube.com/watch?v=ZV-DS_dxilE.

Aleinikoff, T. Alexander (2017b) 'The present, past, and future of refugee protection and solutions: Camps, comprehensive plans, and cyber-communities', *Emory International Law Review*, 31 (4), 539–52.

Aleinikoff, T. Alexander and Leah Zamore (2018) *The arc of protection: Toward a new international refugee regime*, New York: New York University, Public Seminar Books, https://cic.nyu.edu/arc-of-protection-refugees-zamore.

Anastasiadou, Marianthi, Athanasios Marvakis, Panagiota Mezidou and Marc Speer (2017) *From transit hub to dead end: A chronicle of Idomeni*, Munich: bordermonitoring.eu.

Anderson, Benedict (1983) *Imagined communities: Reflections on the origin and spread of nationalism*, London: Verso.

Aristotle, Politics IV. 9, 1294b8, https://en.wikipedia.org/wiki/Sortition#cite_note-7.

Barbelet, Veronique and Christina Bennett (2018) 'Refugia: A place where refugees survive, but do not thrive', *Migration and Society*, 1 (1), 186–89.

Barcelona City Council (2016) 'Barcelona, Refuge City', http://ciutatrefugi.barcelona/en/barcelona-refuge-city.

Bauder, Harald (2017) 'Sanctuary cities: Policies and practices in international perspective', *International Migration*, 55 (2), 174–87.

Bauman, Zigmunt (2000) *Liquid modernity*, Cambridge: Polity.

Bauman, Zigmunt (2007) *Liquid times: Living in an age of uncertainty*, Cambridge: Polity.

BBC News (2016) 'Riace: The Italian village abandoned by locals, adopted by migrants', 26 September, https://www.bbc.co.uk/news/in-pictures-37289713.

BenEzer, Gadi and Roger Zetter (2014) 'Searching for directions: Conceptual and methodological challenges in researching refugee journeys', *Journal of Refugee Studies*, 28 (3), 297–318.

Betts, Alexander, Louise Bloom, Josiah Kaplan and Naohiko Omata (2016) *Refugee economies: Forced displacement and development*, Oxford: Oxford University Press.

Betts, Alexander and Paul Collier (2017) *Refuge: Transforming a broken refugee system*, London: Allen Lane.

Biehl, Kristen Sarah (2014) 'Spatializing diversities, diversifying spaces: Housing experiences and home space perceptions in a migrant hub of Istanbul', *Ethnic and Racial Studies*, 38 (4), 596–607.

Bloch, Ernst (1995/1954–9) *The principle of hope*, Cambridge, MA: MIT Press.

Bloch, Ernst (2000/1918) *The spirit of utopia*, Stanford, CA: Stanford University Press.

Bolleter, Julian and Ken Parish (2019) 'Refuge city: A new kind of city for our times', *The Conversation*, 18 January, https://theconversation.com/refuge-city-a-new-kind-of-city-for-our-times-106992.

Bongie, Chris (1999) 'Reading the archipelago', *New West Indian Guide/Nieuwe West-Indische Gids*, 73 (1/2), 89–95.

Bongie, Chris (2009) 'Edouard Glissant: Dealing in globality' in Charles Forsdick and David Murphy (eds.) *Postcolonial thought in the French-speaking world*, Liverpool: Liverpool University Press, 90–101.

Boochani, Behrouz (2019) 'The Paladin scandal is only a drop in the ocean of corruption on Manus and Nauru', *The Guardian*, 27 February.

Brun, Cathrine and Anita Fábos (2015) 'Making homes in limbo? A conceptual framework', *Refuge*, 31 (1), 5–17.

Brun, Cathrine and Nicholas Van Hear (2012) 'Between the local and the diasporic: The shifting centre of gravity in war-torn Sri Lanka's transnational politics', *Contemporary South Asia*, 20 (1), 61–75.

Buxton, Rebecca, Jade Huynh and Theophilus Kwek (2017) 'Reply to Refugia: Nothing utopian about an archipelago of exclusion', *Refugees Deeply*, 8 November 2017.

Buzi, Jason (2015) 'Refugee nation: A radical solution to the world's refugee crisis', http://www.refugeenation.org/ and https://www.amazon.co.uk/Refugee-Nation-Radical-Solution-Global-ebook/dp/B011JHEBVG.

Cahill, Kevin (2006) *Who owns the world? The hidden facts behind land ownership*, Edinburgh: Mainstream.

Chamoiseau, Patrick (2018) *Migrant brothers: A poet's declaration of human dignity*, New Haven: Yale University Press.

Cohen, Robin (2007) 'Creolization and cultural globalization: The soft sounds of fugitive power', *Globalizations*, 4 (3), 369–84.

Cohen, Robin (2017) *Island societies: Protest and cultural resistance from below*, Oxford: Oxford Publishing Services.

Cohen, Robin (2018) 'Beating the Cambridge Analyticas: Change the way we (s)elect our representatives', https://www.opendemocracy.net/en/author/robin-cohen/.

Cohen, Robin (2019) 'Jude the obscure, updated', http://www.kellogg.ox.ac.uk/blog/jude-the-obscure-updated/.

Cohen, Robin and Paul Kennedy (2013) *Global sociology*, London: Palgrave.

Cohen, Robin and Nicholas Van Hear (2017) 'Visions of Refugia: Territorial and transnational solutions to mass displacement', *Planning Theory & Practice*, 18 (3), 494–504.

Cohen, Robin and Olivia Sheringham (2016) *Encountering difference: Diasporic traces, creolizing spaces*, Cambridge: Polity.

Colau, Ada (2015) 'We, the cities of Europe', http://ajuntament.barcelona.cat/alcaldessa/en/blog/we-cities-europe. Accessed 13 September 2015.

Connelly, Andrew (2016) 'Welcome to the City Plaza: Greece's refugee hotel', *The New Humanitarian/IRIN*, http://www.thenewhumanitarian.org/feature/2016/05/06/welcome-city-plaza-greece-s-refugee-hotel. Accessed June 2019.

Cox, Michael, Gwen Arnold and Sergio Villamayor Tomás (2010) 'A review of design principles for community-based natural resource management', *Ecology and Society*, 15 (4), http://www.ecologyandsociety.org/vol15/iss4/art38/.

Crabapple, Molly (2017) 'This refugee squat represents the best and worst of humanity', *The Guardian*, 23 June.

Crawley, Heaven (2018) 'Why we need to protect refugees from the "big ideas" designed to save them', *The Independent*, Voices (online), 28 July 2018.

Crisp, Jeff (2015) 'Zaatari: A camp and not a city', Refugees International blog post, https://www.refugeesinternational.org/blog/zaatari-camp-and-not-city.

Crisp, Jeff (2018) 'As the world abandons refugees, UNHCR's constraints are exposed', *Refugees Deeply*, 13 September 2018, https://www.newsdeeply.com/refugees/community/2018/09/13/as-the-world-abandons-refugees-unhcrs-constraints-are-exposed.

Crisp, Jeffery (2001) 'Mind the gap! UNHCR, humanitarian assistance and the development process', *International Migration Review*, 35 (1), 168–91.

Daily News and Analysis (2015) 'Egypt billionaire offers to buy island for refugees, wants to name it "Independence"', https://www.dnaindia.com/world/report-egypt-billionare-offers-to-buy-island-for-refugees-wants-to-name-it-independence-2121743.

de Waal, Alex (2014) 'When kleptocracy becomes insolvent: Brute causes of the civil war in South Sudan', *African Affairs*, 113 (452), 347–69.

Devictor, Xavier and Quy-Toan Do (2016) 'How many years do refugees stay in exile?' World Bank blog, http://blogs.worldbank.org/dev4peace/how-many-years-do-refugees-stay-exile. Accessed March 2018.

Dilger, Hansjörg and Kristina Dohrn (eds.) (2016) *Living in refugee camps in Berlin: Women's perspectives and experiences*, Berlin: Weißensee Verlag.

Dong, Qingwen, Kenneth D. Day and Christine M. Collaço (2008) 'Overcoming ethnocentrism through developing intercultural communication sensitivity and multiculturalism', *Human Communication*, 11 (1), 27–38.

Eliassi, Barzoo (2016) 'Statelessness in a world of nation-states: The cases of Kurdish diasporas in Sweden and the UK', *Journal of Ethnic and Migration Studies*, 42 (9), 1403–19.

Elliott, Larry (2018) 'Inequality gap widens as 42 people hold same wealth as 3.7bn poorest', *The Guardian*, 22 January.

Evans, Peter (2008) 'Is an alternative to globalization possible?' *Politics and Society*, 36 (2), 271–305.

Fiddian-Qasmiyeh, Elena (2014) *The ideal refugees: Islam, gender, and the Sahrawi politics of survival*, New York: Syracuse University Press.

Football for Refugees (2017) 'Where we have come from', https://footballforrefugees.com/background/.

Frase, Peter (2016) *Four futures: Visions of the world after capitalism*, London: Verso Books.

Galbraith, John Kenneth (1996) *The good society: The humane agenda*, London: Sinclair-Stevenson.

Giddens, Anthony (1985) *The nation-state and violence*, Berkeley: University of California Press.

Giuffrida, Angela (2018) 'Matteo Salvini orders removal of refugees from Riace', *Guardian*, 15 October.

Glissant, Edouard (1997) *Poetics of relation*, Ann Arbor: University of Michigan Press.

Goldberg, David Theo and John D. Rayner (1989) *The Jewish people: Their history and their religion*, Harmondsworth: Penguin.

Goodhart, David (2017) *The road to Somewhere: The populist revolt and the future of politics*, London: C. Hurst & Co Publishers.

Graham, Mark, Isis Hjorth and Vili Lehdonvirta (2017) 'Digital labour and development: Impacts of global digital labour platforms and the gig economy on worker livelihoods', *Transfer: European Review of Labour and Research*, 23 (2), 135–62.

Halsema, Femke (2016) 'Zatopia', https://www.femkehalsema.nl/zatopia-nergensland/.

Halsema, Femke (2017) *Nergensland: Nieuw licht op migratie*, Amsterdam: Ambo Anthos.

Hamid, Mohsin (2017) *Exit West*, London: Hamish Hamilton.

Hanappe, Cyrille (2017) 'A camp redefined as part of the city', *Forced Migration Review*, 55. www.fmreview.org/shelter/hanappe.html.

Hansen, Bue Rübner and Cameron Thibos (2016) 'Welcoming refugees despite the state', https://www.opendemocracy.net/en/mediterranean-journeys-in-hope/welcoming-refugees-despite-state/.

Hathaway, James C. and Daniel Ghezelbash (2018) 'There's a workable alternative to Australia's asylum policy', *The Guardian*, Opinion, 31 May.

Hathaway, James C. and R. A. Neve (1997) 'Making international refugee law relevant again: A proposal for collectivized and solution-oriented protection', *Harvard Human Rights Journal*, 10, 115–211.

Hicks, Dan and Sarah Mallet (2019) *Lande: The Calais 'jungle' and beyond*, Bristol: Bristol University Press.

Higgins, Michael D. (2012) 'About the Ralahine Centre for Utopian Studies', https://ulsites.ul.ie/ralahinecentre/about-ralahine-centre-utopian-studies.

Jacobsen, Karen (2005) *The economic life of refugees*, West Hartford, CT: Kumarian Press.

Jacobsen, Katja Lindskov (2017) *The politics of humanitarian technology: Good intentions, unintended consequences and insecurity*, London: Routledge.

Kaufmann, Eric (2018) *Whiteshift: Populism, immigration and the future of white majorities*, London: Penguin.

Kay, Diana (1988) 'The politics of gender in exile', *Sociology*, 22 (1), 1–21.

Keating, Joshua (2018) *Invisible countries: Journeys to the edge of nationhood*, New Haven, CT: Yale University Press.

Kleinschmidt, Kilian (2018) 'All cities are refugee camps', https://www.citiestobe.com/kilian-kleinschmidt-all-cities-are-refugee-camps/.

Kleinschmidt, Kilian (2019) 'Cities of tomorrow: From temporariness to inclusion', Prix Bloxhub Interactive, https://prix.bloxhub.org/blog/cities-of-tomorrow-from-temporariness-to-inclusion.

Knapp, Michael, Anja Flach and Ercan Ayboga (2016) *Revolution in Rojava: Democratic autonomy and women's liberation in Syrian Kurdistan*, London: Pluto Press.

Landau, Loren, Kabiri Bule, Ammar Malik, Caroline Wanjiku-Kihato, Yasemin Irvin-Erickson, Benjamin Edwards and Edward Mohr (2017) *Displacement and disconnection? Exploring the role of social networks in the livelihoods of refugees in Gaziantep, Nairobi, and Peshawar*, Washington, DC: Urban Institute.

Lechte, John (2018) 'Rethinking Arendt's theory of necessity: Humanness as "way of life", or: The ordinary as extraordinary', *Theory, Culture and Society*, 35 (1), 3–22.

Leong, Christine (2019) 'D2020: Digital identity with blockchain and biometrics', https://www.accenture.com/us-en/insight-blockchain-id2020.

Lesvos Solidarity (2019) 'Lesvos Solidarity: A year in review', https://drive.google.com/file/d/1OJV4RgszRS8DldvFMjkQijGgyOn58frx/view.

Levitas, Ruth (2013) *Utopia as method: The imaginary reconstitution of society*, Basingstoke: Palgrave.

Limoges, Barrett (2017) 'Thousands of Syrians face eviction from Lebanon camps', *AlJazeera*, 15 April. www.aljazeera.com/indepth/features/2017/04/thousands-syrians-face-eviction-lebanon-camps-170415042553730.html?xif=&c=3729822841203851816&mkt=en-us.

Lindley, Anna (2010) *The early morning phone call: Somali refugees' remittances*, London: Berghahn.

Lippmann, Walter (2004) *The good society*, New York: Routledge.

Loubani, Qusay (2016) 'Small, illegal refugee paradise', openDemocracy, 13 October, www.opendemocracy.net/5050/qusay-loubani/small-illegal-refugee-paradise.

Lowenthal, David (1985) *The past is a foreign country*, Cambridge: Cambridge University Press.

Lutz, Helma (2018) 'Beware of social engineering: A reply to "Refugia" by Nicholas Van Hear', *Migration and Society*, 1 (1), 190–92.

MacBride, Elizabeth (2016) 'Tenacious Egyptian billionaire offers $100 million to help refugees', https://www.forbes.com/sites/elizabethmacbride/2016/05/07/an-egyptian-billionaire-ceo-wants-to-spend-100-million-to-help-refugees-why-is-no-one-listening/#1acbf92d6db2.

Mason, Paul (2015) *PostCapitalism: A guide to our future*, London: Allen Lane.

Mazzara, Federica (2016) 'Subverting the narrative of the Lampedusa borderscape', *Crossings: Journal of Migration and Culture*, 7 (2), 135–47.

Mechelen Declaration (2017) 'The Mechelen Declaration on Cities and Migration', https://www.iom.int/sites/default/files/press_release/file/Mechelen-Declaration-final.pdf.

Menasse, Robert and Ulrike Guérot (2016) 'Europe: The reconstruction of the free world', *Green European Journal*, 12, https://www.greeneuropeanjournal.eu/europe-the-reconstruction-of-the-free-world/.

Miéville, China (2011) *The city and the city*, London: Pan Books.

Misrahi-Barak, Judith and Thomas Lacroix (2019) 'Ecotones: Encounters, crossings, and communities, 2015–2020', Programme outlines, https://emma. www.univ-montp3.fr/fr/valorisation-partenariats/programmes-européens-et-internationaux/ecotones.

More, Thomas (2016/1516) *Utopia*, Edited by George M. Logan. Translated by Robert M. Adams. Cambridge: Cambridge University Press. [First published in Latin in 1516.]

Morris, William (1993/1890) *News from nowhere and other writings*, Harmondsworth: Penguin.

Muggah, Robert and Natalie Sikorski (2018) 'How cities are demanding a greater voice on migration', *Refugees Deeply*, 21 September, https://www.newsdeeply.com/refugees/community/2018/09/21/how-cities-are-demanding-a-greater-voice-on-migration.

Murphy, Joe and Joe Robertson (2018) *The Jungle*, London: Faber and Faber.

Music Action International (2018) 'The music was incredible, and our children had the time of their lives!' https://musicaction.org/syria-summer-school/.

O'Hearn, Denis and Andrej Grubačić (2016) 'Capitalism, mutual aid, and material life: Understanding exilic spaces', *Capital and Class*, 40 (1), 147–65.

Open University (2019) 'The OU outside the UK', http://www.open.ac.uk/about/main/teaching-and-research/ou-outside-uk.

Ostrom, Elinor (2016/1990) *Governing the commons: The evolution of institutions for collective action*, Cambridge: Cambridge University Press.

Pandya, Chhandasi (2006) 'Private authority and disaster relief: The cases of post-tsunami Aceh and Nias, *Critical Asian Studies*, 38 (2), 298–308.

Papadopoulos, Dimitris and Vassilis S. Tsianos (2013) 'After citizenship: Autonomy of migration, organisational ontology and mobile commons', *Citizenship Studies*, 17 (2), 178–96.

Patrikarakos, David (2018) 'Refugees can achieve so much if they're not caged in isolated camps', *The Guardian*, 19 January.

Pickett, Kate and Richard Wilkinson (2009) *The spirit level: Why more equal societies almost always do better*, London: Penguin.

Refugee Republic (2012) refugeerepublic.submarinechannel.com/.

Romer, Paul (2010) 'Technologies, rules, and progress: The case for charter cities', Working Papers id:2471, eSocialSciences, https://ideas.repec.org/p/ess/wpaper/id2471.html.

Rozakou, Katerina (2016) 'Socialities of solidarity: Revisiting the gift taboo in times of crisis', *Social Anthropology*, 24 (2), 185–99.

Rücker, Joachim (2018) 'Sustainable development zones: Tools for economic development for communities in mass displacement scenarios', Los Angeles: Politas Consulting, https://refugeecities.files.wordpress.com/2018/07/sdz-concept-proposal-071118-final.pdf.

Schuck, Peter H. (1997) 'Refugee burden-sharing: A modest proposal', *Yale Journal of International Law*, 22, http://digitalcommons.law.yale.edu/yjil/vol22/iss2/2.

Scott, James (2009) *The art of not being governed: An anarchist history of upland Southeast Asia*, New Haven, CT: Yale University Press.

Shlaim, Avi (2000) *The iron wall: Israel and the Arab world*, London: Allen Lane.

Shuayb, Maha and Cathrine Brun (forthcoming) 'Exceptional and future-less humanitarian education in Lebanon: Prospects for shifting the lens', *Refuge: Canada's Journal on Refugees*.

Sigona, Nando (2015) 'Campzenship: Reimagining the camp as a social and political space', *Citizenship Studies*, 19 (1), 1–15.

Sinclair, Cameron (2018) The ultimate frontier: A regenerative open co-nation and bi-national socio-ecotone, http://cameronsinclair.com/otra.

Solzhenitsyn, Aleksandr (1986) *The Gulag archipelago, 1918–1956*, London: Collins Harvill.

Stone, Peter (2016) 'Sortition, voting, and democratic equality', *Critical Review of International Social and Political Philosophy*, 19 (3), 339–56.

Suhrke, Astri (1998) 'Burden-sharing during refugee emergencies: The logic of collective versus national action', *Journal of Refugee Studies*, 11 (4), 396–415, https://doi.org/10.1093/jrs/11.4.396.

Taylor, Adam (2016) 'A Dutch architect's plan to put Europe's refugees on a man-made island near Tunisia', *Washington Post*, 1 June.

Tolia-Kelly, Divya P. (2018) 'Diaspora and home: Interrogating embodied precarity in an era of forced displacement' in Robin Cohen and Carolin Fischer (eds.) *Routledge handbook of diaspora studies*, London: Routledge, 214–22.

Union of International Associations (UIA) (2012/3) *Yearbook of international organizations*, Leiden: Brill.

United Nations High Commission for Refugees (UNHCR) (2019) *Statistical yearbooks*. Figures at a glance, http://www.unhcr.org/uk/figures-at-a-glance.html, Accessed June 2019.

United Nations Relief and Works Agency (UNRWA) (n.d.) 'Who we are', https://www.unrwa.org/who-we-are.

Van Hear, Nicholas (2018) 'Imagining Refugia: Thinking outside the current refugee regime', *Migration and Society*, 1 (1), 175–85.

Van Hear, Nicholas and Robin Cohen (2017) 'Diasporas and conflict: Distance, contiguity and spheres of engagement', *Oxford Development Studies*, 45 (2), 171–84, https://doi.org/10.1080/13600818.2016.1160043.

van Nieuwkerk, Johannes C. (2018) 'EU-funded refugee incubator villages', 21 August, https://medium.com/@refival/eu-funded-refugee-incubator-villages-e66006ab006a.

Vecchi, Ilaria (2016) 'The experience of the Askavusa Association: Migrant struggle with cultural activities', *Crossings: Journal of Migration and Culture*, 7 (1), 165–79.

Wagner, Lea (2017) 'How can refugees participate in politics?' https://www.bosch-stiftung.de/en/story/how-can-refugees-participate-politics.

Wilson, Alice (2016a) *Sovereignty in Exile: A Saharan liberation movement governs*, Philadelphia, PA: University of Pennsylvania Press.

Wilson, David Sloan (2016b) 'Elinor Ostrom solved one of life's greatest dilemmas: The design principles for solving the tragedy of the commons can be applied to all groups', http://evonomics.com/tragedy-of-the-commons-elinor-ostrom/.

Wimmer, Andreas and Nina Glick Schiller (2002) 'Methodological nationalism and beyond: Nation–state building, migration and the social sciences', *Global Networks*, 2 (4), 301–34.

World Bank (2017) *Cities of Refuge in the Middle East: Bringing an urban lens to the forced displacement challenge*, Policy note, Washington, DC: World Bank.

World Bank (2018) 'Record high remittances to low- and middle-income countries in 2017', http://blogs.worldbank.org/peoplemove/record-high-remittances-low-and-middle-income-countries-2017.

Zak, Danilo (2019) 'Failed pilots: Evaluations of blockchain interventions need transparency', https://www.qeh.ox.ac.uk/blog/failed-pilots-evaluations-blockchain-interventions-need-transparency.

INDEX

Note: Page numbers followed by n refers to notes.

For Product Safety Concerns and Information please contact our EU
representative GPSR@taylorandfrancis.com
Taylor & Francis Verlag GmbH, Kaufingerstraße 24, 80331 München, Germany

www.ingramcontent.com/pod-product-compliance
Lightning Source LLC
Chambersburg PA
CBHW070347270326
41926CB00017B/4023